Hattie
Don't
Play

Jean's Road Trip

Linda

Dot

Betty's Buttermilk

The brown betty *cookbook*

Published by John Wiley & Sons, Inc., Hoboken, New Jersey

Published simultaneously in Canada

Library of Congress Cataloging-in-Publication Data

Brown, Linda Hinton.

  The Brown Betty cookbook : modern vintage desserts from Brown Betty dessert boutique / Linda Hinton Brown and Norrinda Brown Hayat ; photography by Alison Conklin.

     p. cm.

  Includes index.

ISBN 978-1-118-14435-0 (cloth); ISBN 987-1-118-39359-8 (ebk); ISBN 978-1-118-39360-4 (ebk); ISBN 978-1-118-39361-1 (ebk)

  1. Desserts. 2. Cookbooks. I. Hayat, Norrinda Brown. II. Title.

  TX773.B857 2012

  641.86--dc23

                    2011049641

The brown betty cookbook

Modern Vintage Desserts
and Stories

from

Philadelphia's Best Bakery

Linda Hinton Brown *and* Norrinda Brown Hayat

PHOTOGRAPHY BY Alison Conklin

WILEY

John Wiley & Sons, Inc.

CONTENTS

This book, like the bakery, is dedicated to Elizabeth "Betty" Hinton, an old-school domestic goddess, and to the women whose stories Grandmom Betty made come to life during afternoons spent in her kitchen on Frazier Street.

TOGETHER WE WOULD LIKE TO THANK:

Alison Fargis, our agent, without whom this project would have never taken shape and would have stalled on several occasions. Alison is an extraordinary businesswoman who is both affable and unflappable under all circumstances. Justin Schwartz, our editor at Wiley, especially for having the patience to deal with two authors who were emotionally attached to the work and one of whom was also pregnant. We hope you are as happy with the end result as we are. Nicole Paloux, owner of Red Balloon Public Relations, who cheerleaded this project all along the way and introduced us to the wonderfully talented Alison Conklin who photographed the beautiful pictures in this book. Amy Elise Wilson who scouted and styled the most perfect vintage props. Dina Santorelli who edited our personal remembrances with care and at lightning speed. Vanessa Seder who edited our family and bakery recipes. Alicia Nathanson and Adam Suchecki of Blossom Productions who filmed our book trailer. Our hardworking team of bakers, Kevin Murchison, Sarah Schriver and Danielle Ramirez, who keep the bakery's cases stocked daily and who also made the cakes and cupcakes for this book. Our former head decorator, Tessa Brookes Taylor, who poured herself into decorating every single day, and deserves special kudos for frosting the cakes and cupcakes in this book and styling them for the shoot.   The family members who helped fill in the holes in our memories—Aunt Jean, Uncle Buster, Cousins Crystal, Felice, Mary Frances, Karen and Walter. Last, but not least, the Brown Betty customers who have continued to keep our little shops bustling for eight years. We are overflowing with gratitude and humility for the love you have shown our bakeries.

Norrinda would like to give a big thank you to: my dad, Norman, for believing in and supporting every crazy idea that I have ever had including, but not limited to, opening Brown Betty. My sister, Norrina, for being the voice of reason whenever one of those ideas gets too wild and for keeping everything on track. My grandparents, Leon and Elizabeth Hinton and Sallie Marie Renfroe, for being role models on the virtues of hard work, good citizenship and fine character. I keep striving to be like them. My besties— Brandi, Deborah, Jonelle, Khalilah, Lesley, and Maygen who supported Brown Betty in every way possible before we could afford employees and ever since. These sister friends did whatever needed be done for the cause from baking and frosting, to decorating the stores, to reviewing contracts and working the register. My dream catcher, best friend, and husband, Fareed, who has delivered cakes with me up and down the east coast, sat in the bakery for hours on end while I frosted cupcakes and took meetings and who has sacrificed as many days and nights for Brown Betty as I have. You dream big and inspire me to do the same. Kingston, you are the biggest dream your dad helped me catch. Finally, I would like to thank my mom and partner, Linda, for being the backbone of this bakery and joining me on this journey. You are the hardest working person I know and it has been one of the great pleasures of my life to help share your baking genius with the masses.

Linda would like to thank: Brown Betty's very first taste testers, Crystal, Al, and Bashan, for letting me try my recipes out on them the entire summer before we officially opened the bakery. My best friends forever, Esther Arnette and Charmaine Morton, for always being just a phone call away when I needed help with any aspect of Brown Betty. My parents, Leon and Betty Hinton, for passing their love of family, friends, and delicious baking on to the next generation. My daughters, Norrinda and Norrina, for making me a very proud mother. Their unique styles, creativity, and professionalism have led to the success of Brown Betty.

INTRODUCTION

IF YOU WERE TO ASK ME to name my best friend, my favorite person, my closest confidant, when I was eight or ten or twelve years old, I would have undoubtedly answered my grandmom Betty.

I saw her every day. At the time, my family only had one car, and since both my parents worked—my dad owned his own home improvement business, and my mom taught English in the Philadelphia public schools—and my grandparents used public transportation, we would borrow their car. Every morning, my dad would drive us to my grandparents' house, and we would hop into their old 1971 Plymouth Valiant so that my mom could take us to school before she went to work. And in the evenings, we did the reverse—my mom picked us up from school, we drove to my grandparents' home, and we waited there until my dad got home from work and could drive us home. (Years later, even when we had two cars, we still went to Grandmom's in the evenings.) During those visits, I would keep my grandmom

company while she cooked and baked in her kitchen. I would tell her my innocent childhood secrets, and she would share stories of her youth—cracking each other up intermittently between each story.

Weekends were spent with my grandparents too. Every Friday night, we ordered takeout and watched *Dallas* and *Knots Landing* at their house. On Sundays, we would gather there with relatives after church and before going home for dinner. Most often, my grandmom's brothers, Buster and Junior, would also be there, but sometimes others were too—aunts and cousins—and we'd all squeeze in and around the kitchen while my grandmom finished preparing dinner. And again stories would be told. And laughs would be had. There were lots of laughs. This is how I got to know many of my relatives, many of whom passed away years before I was born or when I was very young. Their stories fill the pages of this book.

As I grew older into a teenager and young adult, I spent less and less time in my grandmom's kitchen. Girlfriends, boyfriends, and three-way telephone conversations drew me upstairs into Grandmom's guest bedroom with the door closed, and eventually college and law school beckoned. It was not until years later, after I moved to Washington, D.C., to practice law, that I reflected on how much richer my life had been because of my grandmom and her kitchen. It was during that time that I decided to open a bakery in Philadelphia with my mom, one that paid homage to my first "bestie," Grandmom Betty, and all the other women in our family, whose stories I heard while growing up.

The hardest part was convincing my mom that this was a good idea. All her life, she had simply given away her cakes,

pies, and cookies, and she couldn't imagine people "paying" for them. But once I convinced her, the rest was fairly easy. We already had the family recipes, of course, and my mom had been developing new ones for years, and they were good.

Then fate brought us the perfect location. I had been on a mission to find the smallest footprint possible for the bakery to ensure our monthly expenses were manageable enough for my mom and me to cover them with our salaries, if we needed to. While looking for an apartment in Philadelphia, I stumbled upon Liberties Walk in Northern Liberties. On the tour, the leasing manager described retail space that would eventually be available on the ground floor of the building, and while the apartment didn't work out, we signed a lease for 500 square feet in the development shortly thereafter.

Three tastes test with family and friends later, we opened Brown Betty in the winter of 2004. We had one employee

and two interns manning the store—my mom and I took care of everything else, from mopping the floors to taking out the trash to baking and frosting orders for the following day. Many nights, we took turns sleeping on the pink velvet settee that decorated the bakery's sit-in space, and then in the morning we would head home to get dressed for our day jobs; my mom continued to teach while I worked at a law firm downtown.

That first winter was very long and very hard. At the time, Northern Liberties was not the social scene it is now. There was construction on every corner, and the apartments above us were nowhere near full, so the foot traffic was minimal. What few potential customers there may have been were kept inside by what felt like an endless string of weekend snowstorms, which left us with a refrigerator full of cupcakes on any given Sunday.

I spent the fall and winter writing to all of the local food editors in hopes that a good review would bring traffic to us instead of us waiting for it to stumble in. It wasn't until the following spring, when Kristen Henri, then of *Philadelphia Weekly*, paid us a visit and favorably reviewed our Company's Comin' Coconut Cake that things started looking up. People started to come to Northern Liberties specifically for Brown Betty. Since then, we've been showcased in *O, The Oprah Magazine* (I loved seeing my grandmom's reaction to her full-color photo spread), in *Every Day with Rachael Ray*, on TLC, and on the Food Network, and have received rave reviews in *Glamour*, *National Geographic Traveler*, *Daily Candy*, and every major publication in Philadelphia, including the *Philadelphia Inquirer*, the *Philadelphia Daily News*, *Philadelphia Magazine*, and *City Paper*. Seven years and three stores later, we still have our flagship store in Northern Liberties—we just traded our original 500-square-foot space for another 1,000 square feet a few blocks up on 2nd Street. And we are still turning out cakes, cobblers, and cookies to our hearts' content.

This book is a compilation of the recipes that have made our bakery successful, as well as ones we grew up with, and a few that we thought rounded out the collection. They are all made with the "old school" baking method passed down through four generations, meaning that we only use fresh (never canned) and "real" (butter in our cakes, not margarine) ingredients. We have tried to be as accurate as possible when indicating prep and cooking times (prep times tend to be a bit longer when using fresh produce), so you know what you are getting into before you start a recipe—the last thing you want to do is start preparing the ingredients for Apple Brown Betty when you only have time to squeeze in a quick batch of chocolate chip cookies.

We hope that that these recipes bring your family as much joy as they have brought ours. Perhaps now's the time to begin your own family baking tradition. You've got the recipes to get you started. Now all you need to add is the love and laughter.

FOR AS LONG AS I CAN REMEMBER, my grandmom Betty made the same cake—a plain vanilla pound cake—every weekend. She learned how to make that pound cake as a small girl, in her grandmother's kitchen, and baked it as a new wife, a new grandmother, and well into her seventies until her hands and fingers became too tired to whip and stir anymore.

My mom, Linda, raised in that busy, abundant kitchen, took my grandmom's eighty-year-old recipe and made it a springboard for culinary experimentation, adding pineapple to the batter one time, substituting buttermilk for regular milk another, and over the years she amassed quite a collection of cake recipes of her own.

Today, cakes—pound cakes, in particular—are at the heart of Brown Betty and make up the vast majority of our menu. In this chapter, you'll find recipes that range from Grandmom's vanilla pound cake to those new creations made by Mom, such as Sweet Potato Cake and Cherry Cheesecake, to recipes created specifically for the bakery, including our number one seller, Red Velvet Cake. And we've also included the frosting and filling pairings that we enjoy most. Many of these recipes can be mixed and matched—depending on the season, the occasion, or even your mood—but, most importantly, they're meant to be shared with family and friends.

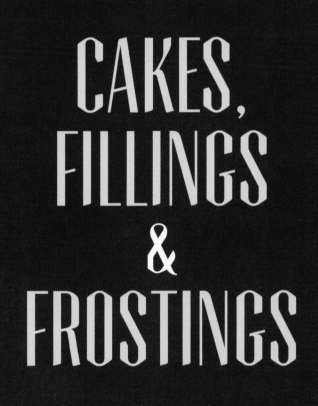

CAKES, FILLINGS & FROSTINGS

BETTY

THERE WAS ALWAYS SOMETHING a little magical about visiting my grandmom on Sundays. We would come straight from church, still dressed in our church clothes, and hungry. My grandmom, often in her starched white uniform from having ushered or served communion, would change as soon as she got home and then go straight to the kitchen to make a snack for anyone who came over and to finish dinner. My grandpop liked consistency, so my grandmom usually cooked the same meal every Sunday—baked chicken, baked or boiled potatoes, and cabbage. You could smell the mix of familiar flavors instantly when you walked into their home. And there were always plenty of baked goods: sweet potato pudding, hard tacks (a country word for "biscuits"), apple pies (two at a time), and Grandmom's famous high, moist pound cakes, which became legendary in our close-knit community.

In fact, long before I came around, from the late 1940s, Grandmom was known throughout West Philadelphia as a gracious hostess and extraordinary baker. As the wife of the chairman of the Deacon Board, which was the center of influence in the church and community at the well-respected Pinn Memorial Baptist Church on Wynnefield Avenue, she was expected to be a member of a number of church organizations, including the Deaconesses, Valkyries, and Ladies Auxiliary. Naturally, that meant Grandmom was always planning a bake sale, luncheon, or fashion show at church, which allowed her ample opportunity to perfect her mile-high pound cake recipe.

Grandmom also entertained a good deal at home. One of the groups of ladies she regularly entertained were her longtime friends from her job at Universal Dental. In the early1950s, Grandmom went to work at Universal Dental in West Philadelphia making dentures. It was considered a plum job at the time, and she was one of literally a few black women hired as a result of the local chapter of the National Association for the Advancement of Colored People's (NAACP) efforts to get the company to integrate. Eventually, Grandmom developed friendships with some of her new coworkers, three of whom were white—a testament to the fact that friendship can transcend color, even during a time when that concept was not a widely held belief.

The girls' working relationship blossomed into genuine personal friendship that would last the rest of their lifetimes. When they were in their thirties and forties, dressed to the nines, they would celebrate special occasions, like birthdays and holidays, together in Atlantic City at the Latin Casino and other supper clubs. As the years passed, the supper clubs and outings to Atlantic City were replaced with rotating dinner parties where all the ladies would go over to each other's homes for a feast that lasted hours. When it was her turn, Grandmom would start preparing a week in advance. She brought out the china and crystal, and Grandpop polished the silver at the kitchen table. Of course, at Grandmom's dinner parties everyone knew the dessert table would be fabulous. And no matter how full the ladies were from dinner, no one could pass up a slice of her delicious pound cake.

My mom, sister, and I would often be there—allegedly to help, but more likely to watch her get ready, since she didn't really need our help. An old-school domestic goddess, she had all of her recipes memorized, and she never let her kitchen get messy.

In addition to the bakery itself, we named our Betty's Buttermilk Pound Cake, which is one of the first recipes my mom ever developed and remains a staple of our bakery, baked fresh every day, after my grandmom. Magic, we've decided, shouldn't be reserved just for Sundays.

PLAIN CAKE

This is the grandmother of Brown Betty pound cakes, the recipe from which all other recipes are derived. At least one hundred years old, it is the cake that I watched my grandmom Betty make every weekend until I went away to college and the cake she watched her own grandmother make decades before. Betty had the recipe memorized, and amazingly it came out perfectly every time—mile high, light, and moist.

Serves: 20 people

1 Preheat the oven to 350°F. Coat a 10-inch angel food cake pan with nonstick cooking spray.

2 In a medium bowl, whisk together the flour, baking powder, and salt.

3 In the bowl of a stand mixer fitted with the paddle attachment, beat the butter until light and fluffy and the add sugar on low speed until the mixture is light and fluffy, scraping the bowl as necessary, about 3 minutes. Add the eggs, 1 at a time, beating until blended and scraping the bowl occasionally.

4 In a measuring cup, mix the milk and vanilla together. Reduce the mixer speed to low and alternately add the flour mixture and milk mixture to the butter mixture, beginning and ending with the

Active time:
30 minutes

Total time:
1 hour and 45 minutes

Nonstick cooking spray with flour

4 cups cake flour

1¾ teaspoons baking powder

¾ teaspoon regular salt

4 sticks (2 cups) unsalted butter, at room temperature

3 cups granulated sugar

8 large eggs

¾ cup whole milk

1½ teaspoons pure vanilla extract

Pinch of ground nutmeg

1 recipe (about 3 cups) Vanilla Buttercream (recipe follows) or Tea Buttercream (see page 23)

flour mixture and beating until smooth. Scrape the bowl. Add the nutmeg and beat until blended.

5 Pour the batter into the prepared pan and bake until a wooden pick inserted near the center comes out clean, 70 to 75 minutes. Let the cake cool in the pan for 10 minutes before turning it out onto a wire rack to cool completely.

6 To frost the cake, turn it bottom-side up onto a cake plate. Using an offset spatula, spread the buttercream all over the cake.

VANILLA BUTTERCREAM

Makes: 4 cups

1 In the bowl of a stand mixer fitted with the paddle attachment, beat the cream cheese and vanilla together on medium speed until smooth, about 3 minutes. Add the butter and salt and beat, scraping the bowl as necessary, until mixed.

2 Reduce the mixer speed to low and gradually add the confectioners' sugar, beating until blended. Increase the mixer speed to high and beat until light and fluffy, about 2 minutes. Set aside until ready to use.

Active time:
12 minutes

Total time:
20 minutes

6 ounces Philadelphia® cream cheese, at room temperature

2 teaspoons pure vanilla extract

2 sticks (1 cup) unsalted butter, at room temperature

Pinch of regular salt

3½ cups confectioners' sugar

TEA BUTTERCREAM

There was a great tea shop named "Remedy Tea Bar" in Philly that opened right around the time we did. We baked cupcakes for the shop for a while, and thought it would be neat to create tea-flavored buttercreams. We developed green tea and Earl Grey buttercream for our plain cupcakes and chai for chocolate cupcakes, but the way the recipe is written, any flavored tea is possible.

Makes: 4 cups

Active time:
25 minutes

Total time:
40 minutes,
plus brewing time

3 tablespoons loose-leaf tea, such as chai, green, or Earl Grey

¾ cup water

2 ounces Philadelphia® cream cheese, at room temperature

5 sticks (2½ cups) unsalted butter, at room temperature

3 large egg yolks

¾ cup granulated sugar

6 tablespoons light corn syrup

Vegetable shortening, for greasing

1 In a small microwave-safe bowl, combine the tea with ½ cup water. Microwave on high until the liquid boils. Cover with plastic wrap and leave out overnight.

2 The next day, use a fine-mesh strainer to strain the tea into a small bowl. The strained tea should equal ¼ cup.

3 In the bowl of a stand mixer fitted with the paddle attachment, beat the cream cheese on medium speed until light and fluffy, about 3 minutes. Reduce the mixer speed to low, add the butter, and beat until blended. Increase the mixer speed to medium-high and beat until the mixture doubles in volume, scraping the bowl occasionally, 4 to 6 minutes.

4 Meanwhile, use a hand mixer on high speed to beat the egg yolks in a large bowl until pale, about 3 minutes.

5 In a medium saucepan over low heat, stir the sugar, corn syrup, and the remaining ¼ cup of water until the sugar has dissolved. Continue to cook until the mixture is clear and comes to a boil. Pour this mixture into a lightly greased glass measuring cup.

6 Slowly drizzle the sugar syrup into the egg yolks while mixing on medium speed. Once blended, increase the speed to high and beat until light and fluffy, scraping the bowl occasionally, about 5 minutes.

7 Add the tea to the egg yolk mixture and beat on high speed for 5 minutes, until blended. Pour the egg yolk mixture into a clean mixing bowl.

8 Add half of the whipped cream cheese–butter to the egg yolk mixture and beat on medium speed until blended. Add the remaining whipped cream cheese–butter and beat on high speed until light and fluffy, scraping the bowl occasionally, about 5 minutes. Use immediately or refrigerate in an airtight container until ready to use.

RUTH

GRANDMOM'S MOTHER, RUTH, DIED when my grandmother and her brothers were very young—Grandmom was only two years old, Uncle Buster was a newborn, and her brother, Christopher, nicknamed "Junior," was only one. Medical records being what they were in the early 1900s, it is difficult to say for certain from what malady Ruth suffered, but we know she became ill during childbirth with Uncle Buster (as did Buster, who remained sickly for much of his childhood) and then simply could not recover.

Because she was only a toddler, Grandmom doesn't remember much about her mother, but throughout her life Ruth took on a very powerful spiritual role. What we know of her comes from bits and pieces of memories, often culled from stories at the dinner table, which have been passed down across the generations.

Ruth and her husband, Christopher "Woody" Gaskins Sr., lived next door to Ruth's brother, Thomas, and his wife, Eva, on the 4800 block of Olive Street in West Philadelphia. As the story goes, Ruth once told Eva that if anything ever happened to her, she could raise Buster, since Eva could not have any children of her own, and when Ruth died, Eva did keep Buster for a while to help out. Although he ultimately went back to live with his father and siblings, having Eva next door was a huge influence on all of the children's lives.

Like her sister, Mary Evans, Ruth had her beauty license, but she was allergic to the smoke—the iron straightening combs and curling irons often emitted a lot of smoke—and the doctor told her that she "shouldn't do hair." So instead she worked for a real estate company.

What everyone remembers most about Ruth was her fashion sense. Tall and shapely, she belonged to a club in town that would have her model clothing, and she would walk the local catwalks—at church functions and other community gatherings—to the delight of her family.

Ruth is remembered as outgoing and friendly, with lots of friends. She served as an usher at the Pinn Memorial Baptist Church in Philadelphia, and following Sunday service she would often attend all kinds of dinners at the homes of friends and family for which she would bake cakes, apple pies, and rice and bread pudding.

Throughout their lives, Grandmom and her brothers often wondered what life would have been like if they had been able to grow up with their mother, but when I think of Ruth, I imagine her as always being there, somewhere, in her fancy clothes, watching and protecting her babies as they grew up and made new babies to love and nurture. We named our chocolate sour cream cake "Dear Ruth" as a dedication to a woman who may not have lived in her children's memories, but continued to live in their hearts.

DEAR RUTH

Chocolate Sour Cream Cake with Chocolate Buttercream

This is our updated version of chocolate diner cake. The chocolate—we use unsweetened Dutch-process cocoa powder mixed with traditional cocoa powder—is not too dark (for the kids), but not too light (for the big kids). It has a bit of gooeyness, and because we separate four petite layers with a chocolate buttercream, the cake to buttercream ratio is more evenly divided. And we finish it off with chocolate curls around the sides to keep it true to its diner roots.

Serves: 20 people

1 Preheat the oven to 350°F. Coat two 9-inch round cake pans with vegetable shortening, line the bottoms of the pans with parchment paper, and spray with nonstick cooking spray.

2 In a medium bowl, mix together the sour cream, cocoa powder, eggs, egg yolks, and vanilla until smooth.

3 In the bowl of a stand mixer fitted with the paddle attachment, beat the flour, baking powder, baking soda, salt, and sugar on low speed just until blended. Add the butter and half of the cocoa mixture to the flour mixture and beat until the dry ingredients are moist.

Active time:
30 minutes

Total time:
60 minutes

Vegetable shortening

Nonstick cooking spray with flour

¾ cup sour cream

½ cup plus 3 tablespoons cocoa powder (equal parts unsweetened cocoa powder and Dutch- process cocoa)

2 large eggs

2 large egg yolks

1½ teaspoons pure vanilla extract

2¼ cups cake flour

1 teaspoon baking powder

1 teaspoon baking soda

¾ teaspoon regular salt

1¾ cups granulated sugar

2 sticks (1 cup) unsalted butter, at room temperature

½ cup boiling water

continued on the following page

4 Increase the mixer speed to medium and beat until smooth, about 2 minutes. Gradually add the remaining cocoa mixture in 2 batches, beating well after each addition. Add ½ cup boiling water and beat until smooth.

5 Divide the batter equally between the prepared pans and smooth the tops with an offset spatula. Bake until a wooden pick inserted into the center comes out clean, 30 to 35 minutes. Let the cakes cool in the pans for 10 minutes before turning them out onto a wire rack to cool completely. Remove the parchment paper.

6 Use a large serrated knife to cut each of the 2 layers in half to make 4 layers total. Place the first layer on a cake plate. Use an offset spatula to spread 1 cup of the buttercream on top, and then repeat with the next 2 layers. Place the final cake layer on top and spread the remaining buttercream on the top and sides of the cake. Cover the sides of the cake with dark chocolate curls, if desired.

continued from page 29

2 recipes Chocolate Buttercream (see page 91)

Dark chocolate curls, for garnish (optional)

BETTY'S BUTTERMILK POUND CAKE

Lemon Cake with Lemon Buttercream

This is one of the original recipes that my mom developed, long before we opened the bakery, when she was still tearing out recipes from magazines over summer vacation. But it was one of the cakes that convinced me we should open a bakery in the first place. Today, it's one of our staples. Made with buttermilk and a hint of fresh lemon juice in the batter, this cake is fitting for any occasion. Eat it plain, frosted, or, if you are having people over like Betty often did, try it lightly toasted with strawberries and fresh whipped cream.

Serves: 20 people

1 Preheat the oven to 350°F. Coat a 10-inch angel food cake pan with nonstick cooking spray.

2 In a large bowl, whisk together the flour, salt, baking powder, and baking soda.

3 In the bowl of a stand mixer fitted with the paddle attachment, beat the butter until light and fluffy and then add the sugar on low speed until smooth, scraping the bowl as necessary, about 2 minutes. Add the eggs, 1 at a time, beating until blended and

Active time:
30 minutes

Total time:
1 hour and 45 minutes

Nonstick cooking spray with flour

4½ cups all-purpose flour

1 teaspoon regular salt

¾ teaspoon baking powder

¾ teaspoon baking soda

3 sticks (1½ cups) unsalted butter, at room temperature

3 cups superfine sugar

8 large eggs, at room temperature

1½ teaspoons pure vanilla extract

1½ teaspoons fresh lemon juice

¼ teaspoon pure lemon extract

1¼ cups buttermilk

1 recipe Lemon Buttercream (recipe follows)

scraping the bowl occasionally. Beat in the vanilla extract, lemon juice, and lemon extract.

4 Reduce the mixer speed to low and alternately add the flour mixture, 1 cup at a time, and buttermilk, ¼ cup at a time, to the butter mixture, mixing until well incorporated.

5 Spread the batter into the prepared pan and bake until golden brown on top and a wooden pick inserted near the center comes out clean, 60 minutes. Let the cake cool in the pan for 10 minutes before turning the cake out onto a wire rack to cool completely.

6 To frost the cake, turn it bottom-side up onto a cake plate. Using an offset spatula, spread the frosting all over the cake.

LEMON BUTTERCREAM

Makes: 3 cups

1 In the bowl of a stand mixer fitted with the paddle attachment, beat the cream cheese on medium speed until smooth, about 3 minutes.

2 Add the butter, lemon extract, and salt to the cream cheese and beat until fluffy, scraping the bowl as necessary, about 3 minutes. Gradually add the confectioner's sugar, beating until blended and scraping the bowl occasionally.

3 Gradually add enough of the lemon juice to achieve a spreadable consistency. Increase the mixer speed to high and beat until the frosting is fluffy, about 1 minute. Set aside until ready to use.

Active time:
12 minutes

Total time:
18 minutes

- 2 ounces Philadelphia® cream cheese, at room temperature
- 1 stick (8 tablespoons) unsalted butter, at room temperature
- ¼ teaspoon pure lemon extract
- Pinch of regular salt
- 2½ cups confectioners' sugar
- 2 tablespoons fresh lemon juice

SALLIE MARIE'S SOUR CREAM POUND CAKE

This is the pretty cake that we had photographed for *O, The Oprah Magazine* in 2007. The picture came out so pretty that everyone—even the magazine editors—wanted to know what kind of cake it was. Turns out, it's just vanilla pound cake. Who says vanilla has to be boring? But if you are looking for a real show piece, you can always bake this cake in three layer pans instead of an angel food pan and use either the lemon or raspberry curd recipes that follow as fillings in between each layer.

Serves: 20 people

1 Preheat the oven to 350°F. Coat a 10-inch angel food cake pan with nonstick cooking spray.

2 In a medium bowl, whisk together the flour, salt, baking powder, and baking soda.

3 In the bowl of a stand mixer fitted with the paddle attachment, beat the butter until light and fluffy and then add the sugar on low speed until smooth, scraping the bowl as necessary, about 3 minutes. Add the eggs, 1 at a time, beating until blended. Add the vanilla and rum extracts and beat until blended.

Active time:
30 minutes

Total time:
1 hour and 45 minutes

Nonstick cooking spray with flour

4 cups cake flour

¾ teaspoon regular salt

½ teaspoon baking powder

¼ teaspoon baking soda

3 sticks (1½ cups) unsalted butter, at room temperature

3 cups granulated sugar

8 large eggs

1½ teaspoons pure vanilla extract

¼ teaspoon pure rum extract

1 cup sour cream

1 recipe (about 3 cups) Vanilla Buttercream (see page 22) or Chocolate Buttercream (see page 91)

4 Reduce the mixer speed to low and alternately
   add the flour mixture and sour cream to the butter
   mixture, beginning and ending with the flour mixture
   and beating until smooth.

5 Pour the batter into the prepared pan and bake until
   a wooden pick inserted near the center comes out
   clean, 60 minutes. Let the cake cool in the pan for
   10 minutes before turning it out onto a wire rack to
   cool completely.

6 To frost the cake, turn it bottom-side up onto a cake
   plate. Using an offset spatula, spread the buttercream
   all over the cake.

LEMON AND RASPBERRY CURD

No matter where I live, I really am a Philly girl at heart. I grew up on Jim's cheesesteaks,
Frank's sodas, Overbrook water ice and soft pretzels, and Tastykake jelly krimpets and
lemon-filled pies. When we started filling our sour cream cupcakes with lemon and
raspberry curd, it brought to mind those favorite childhood treats. Now, whenever I
taste these fillings, it is almost like I am twelve again.

LEMON CURD

Makes: 1 cup

1 In the bowl of a stand mixer fitted with the paddle attachment, beat the eggs, egg yolks, and sugar on medium speed until well blended and fluffy.

2 In a medium saucepan over medium-low heat, combine the egg mixture, lemon juice, butter, salt, and zest and cook, stirring constantly, until thickened but not boiling. The mixture should be thick enough to coat a wooden spoon, but still pourable.

3 If you're not using the curd immediately, transfer it to a medium bowl and cool to room temperature. Cover the surface directly with plastic wrap to prevent a skin from forming. Refrigerate in an airtight container until ready to use or up to 7 days.

Active time:
20 minutes

Total time:
35 minutes

2 large eggs

4 large egg yolks

½ cup plus 2 tablespoons granulated sugar

6 tablespoons fresh lemon juice

½ stick (4 tablespoons) unsalted butter

Pinch of regular salt

2 teaspoons freshly grated lemon zest

RASPBERRY CURD

Makes: 2 cups

Active time:
35 minutes

Total time:
45 minutes

24 ounces fresh or frozen raspberries

1 stick (8 tablespoons) unsalted butter

1½ teaspoons fresh lemon juice

Pinch of regular salt

8 large egg yolks

4 large eggs

1¼ cups granulated sugar

1½ teaspoons cornstarch

1 Using a food processor, pulse the raspberries until smooth. Push the raspberry purée through a fine-mesh strainer into a medium bowl to remove the seeds. Repeat the process until almost all the seeds are removed.

2 In a medium saucepan, combine 1½ cups of the purée, butter, lemon juice, and salt.

3 In the bowl of a stand mixer fitted with the whisk attachment, whisk the egg yolks, eggs, sugar, and cornstarch on medium speed until well blended and fluffy. Add the egg mixture to the raspberry mixture in the saucepan and stir to blend.

4 Cook over medium heat, stirring constantly, until thickened. The mixture should change to a darker color and be thick enough to coat a spoon but still pourable.

5 If you're not using the curd immediately, transfer it to a medium bowl and cool to room temperature. Cover the surface directly with plastic wrap to prevent a skin from forming. Refrigerate in an airtight container until ready to use or up to 7 days.

A WORD ON CUPCAKES

To be sure, Brown Betty is a bakery and not a cupcakery, but there is no denying the popularity of our cupcakes. The secret? Our cupcakes are really small versions of our delicious cakes. So if an occasion arises where only a cupcake or a couple dozen will do, you can make cupcakes out of any of the batters in the book (all of the batters in this book should make at least 20 cupcakes). All you need is a cupcake pan and some cupcake liners. Remember, cupcakes need to bake for less time than a cake—23 to 24 minutes at 350°F. Finally, don't forget that one of the most enjoyable parts of making cupcakes is how much fun you can have frosting them. We suggest playing around with food coloring to turn that vanilla frosting hot pink, or using sprinkles to add a bit of pizzazz to chocolate. Let your imagination and the occasion guide you.

ALICE'S TWO-STEP

Almond Pound Cake with Caramel Buttercream

Whenever there was a birthday celebrated on my dad's side of the family, there would always be a cake from Eiselen's, an old-school Italian American bakery in the Roxborough neighborhood of Philadelphia. The bakery had only two flavors, vanilla and chocolate, and decorated every cake the same way, with white icing and any-color-you-wanted piped roses. But the cake inside was delicious, and I could never quite put my finger on what made the vanilla taste so unique— that is, until one of our bakers asked us to develop an "almond cake" for her wedding. As soon as we tasted the first run, we knew that all-too-familiar flavor and suspected Eiselen's secret vanilla ingredient—a hint of almond. We added the cake to the menu and eventually decided to take it up a notch and put a caramel buttercream with it. Delicious. We think of it as "old school meets new school."

Serves: 20 people

1 Preheat the oven to 350°F. Line three 9-inch round cake pans with parchment paper and lightly spray with nonstick cooking spray.

2 In a medium bowl, whisk together the flour, baking powder, and salt.

Active time:
30 minutes

Total time:
1 hour and 45 minutes

Nonstick cooking spray with flour

4 cups cake flour

1¾ teaspoons baking powder

¾ teaspoon regular salt

4 sticks (2 cups) unsalted butter, at room temperature

3 cups superfine sugar

8 large eggs, at room temperature

¾ cup whole milk

2 teaspoons pure almond extract

½ teaspoon pure vanilla extract

1 recipe Caramel Buttercream (recipe follows)

Salted pretzel pieces, for garnish

3 In the bowl of a stand mixer fitted with the paddle attachment, beat the butter until light and fluffy and then add the sugar on low speed until smooth, about 3 minutes. Increase the mixer speed to medium and add the eggs, 1 at a time, beating until blended and scraping the bowl occasionally.

4 In a small bowl, mix the milk, almond extract, and vanilla extract together. Reduce the mixer speed to low and alternately add the flour mixture and the milk mixture to the butter mixture, beginning and ending with the flour mixture and mixing just until incorporated.

5 Divide the batter equally among the prepared pans and bake until a wooden pick inserted into the center comes out clean, 30 to 35 minutes. Let the cakes cool in the pans for 10 minutes before turning them out onto a wire rack to cool completely. Remove the parchment paper from the cakes.

6 To assemble and frost the cakes, place 1 cake layer, bottom-side up, on a cake plate. Use an offset spatula to spread 1 cup of the buttercream on top. Add the second cake layer, bottom-side down, and spread 1 cup of the buttercream on top. Top with the third cake layer, bottom-side up. Frost the top and sides of the cake with the remaining buttercream. Garnish with the salted pretzel pieces.

CARAMEL BUTTERCREAM

Makes: 3½ cups

1 In the bowl of a stand mixer fitted with the paddle attachment, beat the cream cheese on medium speed until light and fluffy, about 3 minutes. Reduce the mixer speed to low, add the butter, and beat until blended. Increase the mixer speed to medium-high and beat until the mixture is pale yellow and doubles in volume, scraping the bowl occasionally, 4 to 6 minutes.

2 Meanwhile, use a hand mixer on high speed to beat the egg yolks in a large bowl until pale, about 3 minutes.

3 In a medium saucepan over low heat, stir the sugar, corn syrup, and ¼ cup water until the sugar has dissolved. Continue to cook until the mixture is clear and comes to a boil. Pour this mixture into a lightly greased glass measuring cup.

4 Slowly drizzle the sugar syrup into the egg yolks while mixing on medium speed. Once blended, increase the speed to high and beat until light and fluffy, scraping the bowl occasionally, about 5 minutes.

Active time:
30 minutes

Total time:
30 minutes

2 ounces Philadelphia® cream cheese, at room temperature

5 sticks (2½ cups) unsalted butter, cut into small pieces, at room temperature

¾ cup superfine sugar

6 tablespoons light corn syrup

¼ cup water

3 large egg yolks

Vegetable shortening, for greasing

1 cup Caramel Sauce (recipe follows)

5 Add the caramel sauce to the egg yolk mixture and whisk on high speed for 5 minutes. Pour the egg mixture into a clean glass bowl.

6 Add half of the whipped cream cheese–butter to the egg yolk mixture and beat on medium speed until blended. Add the remaining whipped cream cheese–butter and beat on high speed until light and fluffy, scraping the bowl occasionally, about 5 minutes. Use immediately or refrigerate in an airtight container until ready to use.

Caramel Sauce

Makes: 1 cup

Active time:
30 minutes

Total time:
18 minutes

¾ cup superfine sugar

6 tablespoons light corn syrup

¼ cup water

Pinch of regular salt

½ cup heavy cream

½ teaspoon pure vanilla extract

1 In a heavy medium saucepan over medium heat, combine the sugar, corn syrup, ¼ cup water, and salt. Bring to a simmer, stirring occasionally, until the sugar dissolves. Reduce the heat to low and simmer without stirring until it turns a golden color.

2 Remove the saucepan from the heat, add the cream and vanilla, and stir until thoroughly blended, about 1 minute. Allow the sauce to cool to room temperature. The sauce will thicken as it cools. Set aside until ready to use.

ELIZA

Grandmom was five years old when she and her brothers moved from Philadelphia to Tappahannock to live with their paternal grandmother, Eliza Gaskins, who raised them well into their teens.

The family lived on a farm in the country, about seven miles out of town, a veritable wonderland for the three siblings who had been unaccustomed to such wide, open spaces. With long, flowing tresses, Eliza was a cute, petite woman—not slender, but curvy—and her husband, George, like most men in his day, didn't believe his wife should be working outside, tilling the soil in the strong Virginia sun. So, inside Eliza stayed, mostly in her kitchen, and while the boys busied themselves with the land, it was there that she taught Grandmom everything she knows about cooking and baking.

Although her childhood spanned the Great Depression, Grandmom remembers those years as a time of abundance, when food, and ingredients, were plentiful. The family grew corn, watermelons, cabbage, greens, tomatoes, squash, and other vegetables and raised pigs, cows, and chickens, which provided a stable supply of meat, milk, and eggs. They churned their own butter and made lard from the hog fat, and there were barrels, not boxes, of flour, from which to draw. As Uncle Buster often said, "Eliza fed us good. Real good."

Eliza fed lots of people in those days. She was a gentle, compassionate soul whose door was open to anyone who cared to walk through it. And they often did.

Family. Friends. Neighbors. Strangers. Everyone was welcome at Eliza's. Folks dropped by for meals or to take food out with them if they were unable to stay. Some, if they could, would offer Eliza money as a token of their appreciation, which she would gladly take so she could buy more ingredients for the next meal she aimed to fix.

Often Grandmom or her brothers would bring home children they knew were homeless or who lived in foster homes and needed a decent, home-cooked meal. Eliza never turned anybody down. For years, I've heard the story about "Blind Jim," the town vagabond who just "happened" to walk by Eliza's house during mealtimes. Like clockwork. Eliza would call out to the children and say, "Go get him, and make sure he washes up." And each time, they would escort Blind Jim to the bathroom, give him some soap and a towel, and then bring him to the table. After his meal, they'd escort him back to the exact spot outside where they had found him, so he could continue on his way. "Blind Jim may have been blind," Grandmom always says with a laugh, "but he could always tell when it was time to come and get his lunch."

It was that small farm kitchen, where kindness flowed as generously as the ingredients, and the servings, where my Grandmom became the person she is—not only an exceptional cook and baker, but a caring and compassionate person who is as generous with her time and knowledge as her grandmother had been. And because the taste of our specialty sweet potato pound cake relies so much on sugar and spice, we made sure to name it for Eliza to provide the everything nice.

ONLY FOR ELIZA

Sweet Potato Cake with Spiced Vanilla Buttercream

I had nothing to do with the development of this cake. In fact, I stood in silent opposition to its creation for fear we had "too much sweet potato on the menu already." I admit it: I was wrong. The puréed sweet potato makes the batter so moist and, paired with a spiced vanilla buttercream that has just the right amount of complexity, this cake is like no other on our menu. It is my new favorite and has been rivaling red velvet as our number one seller since its introduction.

Serves: 20 (or more) people

---

1 Preheat the oven to 350°F. Coat three 9-inch round cake pans with nonstick cooking spray and line a rimmed baking sheet with foil.

2 Place the potatoes on the baking sheet and rub the skins with oil. Roast the potatoes until tender when pierced with a fork, 50 to 55 minutes. Set the potatoes aside until they are cool enough to handle. Using a knife, remove the skin of the sweet potatoes and place the flesh of the potatoes in the bowl of a stand mixer fitted with the paddle attachment. Beat the potato flesh on medium-high speed to remove pulp, about 1 minute. Push the flesh through a fine-mesh strainer over a medium bowl. Set aside.

Active time:
1 hour and 25 minutes

Total time:
1 hour and 55 minutes

Nonstick cooking spray with flour

1½ pounds sweet potatoes or yams, scrubbed

2 tablespoons vegetable oil

4 cups all-purpose flour

2 teaspoons baking soda

1 teaspoon baking powder

¾ teaspoon regular salt

1⅛ teaspoons ground cinnamon

½ teaspoon ground nutmeg

⅛ teaspoon ground ginger

3 sticks (1½ cups) unsalted butter, at room temperature

2 cups granulated sugar

½ cup packed light brown sugar

8 large eggs

continued on the following page

3 In a medium bowl, whisk together the flour, baking soda, baking powder, salt, cinnamon, nutmeg, and ginger.

4 In the bowl of a stand mixer fitted with the paddle attachment, beat the butter, granulated sugar, and brown sugar on medium speed until light and fluffy, scraping the bowl as necessary, about 3 minutes. Add the eggs, 1 at a time, beating until blended. Add the strained sweet potatoes and vanilla and beat until blended.

5 Reduce the mixer speed to low and alternately add the flour mixture and evaporated milk to the sweet potato mixture, beginning and ending with the flour mixture and beating until smooth.

6 Divide the batter equally among the prepared pans and bake until a wooden pick inserted into the center comes out clean, 25 to 30 minutes. Let the cakes cool in the pans for 10 minutes before turning them out onto a wire rack to cool completely.

7 To assemble and frost the cakes, place 1 cake layer, bottom-side up, on a cake plate. Use an offset spatula to spread 1 cup of the buttercream on top. Add the second cake layer, bottom-side down, and spread 1 cup of the buttercream on top. Top with the third cake layer, bottom-side up. Frost the top and sides of the cake with the remaining buttercream.

continued from page 49

1 ½ teaspoons pure vanilla extract

1 cup evaporated milk

1 recipe Spiced Vanilla Buttercream (recipe follows)

SPICED VANILLA BUTTERCREAM

Active time:
12 minutes

Total time:
20 minutes

Makes: 4 cups

1 In the bowl of a stand mixer fitted with the paddle attachment, beat the cream cheese and vanilla together on medium speed until fluffy, about 3 minutes. Add the butter and salt and beat until blended, scraping the bowl as necessary.

2 Reduce the mixer speed to low and gradually add the confectioner's sugar, beating until blended. Scrape the bowl and add the cinnamon. Increase the mixer speed to high and beat until light and fluffy, about 1 minute. Set aside until ready to use.

- 6 ounces Philadelphia® cream cheese, at room temperature
- 2 teaspoons pure vanilla extract
- 2 sticks (1 cup) unsalted butter, at room temperature
- Pinch of regular salt
- 14 ounces (1¾ cups) confectioners' sugar
- ½ teaspoon ground cinnamon

STRAWBERRY LETTER

Strawberry Pound Cake with Strawberry Buttercream

I love this strawberry cake so much that we flew it across country to California for my wedding. Named one of the five best cupcakes in the country by *Every Day with Rachael Ray*, our Strawberry Letter is a pretty cake with a light pink tint. We purée whole strawberries and add them to both the cake and the buttercream to create little specks of red throughout each layer. It is especially lovely for summertime parties.

Serves: 20 people

---

1 Preheat the oven to 350°F. Coat three 9-inch round cake pans with nonstick cooking spray.

2 Mash the strawberries through a strainer over a measuring cup until you get 1 cup of juice. Reserve the mashed strawberries. Add the 1 cup of juice to a saucepan. Bring to a boil and cook until reduced to ¼ cup.

3 Using a food processor, pulse the reserved mashed strawberries until they are finely chopped. Add the reduced strawberry juice and lemon juice to the chopped strawberries and pulse until blended. Set aside.

Active time:
30 minutes

Total time:
1 hour and 5 minutes

Nonstick cooking spray with flour

16 ounces frozen strawberries, thawed

1½ teaspoons fresh lemon juice

4 cups cake flour

1¾ teaspoons baking powder

¾ teaspoon regular salt

4 sticks (2 cups) unsalted butter, at room temperature

3 cups granulated sugar

6 large eggs

2 large egg yolks

1½ teaspoons strawberry liqueur

¼ teaspoon red food coloring

¼ cup whole milk

1 recipe Strawberry Buttercream (recipe follows)

4 In a medium bowl, whisk together the flour, baking powder, and salt.

5 In the bowl of a stand mixer fitted with the paddle attachment, beat the butter until light and fluffy and then add the sugar on low speed until smooth. Add the eggs and egg yolks, 1 at a time, beating until blended. Add ¾ cup of the strawberry purée, the liqueur, and the red food coloring to the batter and beat until incorporated.

6 Reduce the mixer speed to low and alternately add the flour mixture, 1 cup at a time, and the milk, 2 tablespoons at a time, to the butter mixture, beating until smooth.

7 Divide the batter equally among the prepared pans and bake until a wooden pick inserted into the middle comes out clean, 30 to 35 minutes. Let the cakes cool in the pans for 10 minutes before turning them out onto a wire rack to cool completely.

8 To assemble and frost the cakes, place 1 cake layer, bottom-side up, on a cake plate. Use an offset spatula to spread 1 cup of the buttercream on top. Add the second cake layer, bottom-side down, and spread 1 cup of the buttercream on top. Top with the third cake layer, bottom-side up. Frost the top and sides of the cake with the remaining buttercream.

STRAWBERRY BUTTERCREAM

Active time: 30 minutes

Total time: 45 minutes

Makes: 4 cups

16 ounces frozen strawberries, thawed

1½ teaspoons fresh lemon juice

4 ounces Philadelphia® cream cheese, at room temperature

1 teaspoon strawberry liqueur

2 sticks (1 cup) unsalted butter, at room temperature

Pinch of regular salt

10 ounces (1¼ cups) confectioners' sugar

1 Mash the strawberries through a strainer over a measuring cup until you get 1 cup of juice. Reserve the mashed strawberries. Add the 1 cup of juice to a saucepan. Bring to a boil and cook until reduced to ¼ cup.

2 Using a food processor, pulse the reserved mashed strawberries until they are finely chopped. Add the reduced strawberry juice and lemon juice to the chopped strawberries and pulse until blended. Set aside.

3 In the bowl of a stand mixer fitted with the paddle attachment, beat the cream cheese and strawberry liqueur on medium speed until soft. Add the butter and salt and beat until light and fluffy, scraping the bowl as necessary, about 3 minutes. Reduce the mixer speed to low, add ⅛ cup of the strawberry purée to the butter mixture, and beat until just blended.

4 Gradually beat in the confectioner's sugar, scraping the bowl occasionally, until well blended. Increase the mixer speed to high and beat until the buttercream is fluffy, about 1 minute. Refrigerate until ready to use.

CARROT PATCH

Carrot Cake with White Chocolate Buttercream and Cream Cheese Frosting

There may be nothing worse than dry carrot cake. That's why we add lots of freshly shredded carrots and rum-soaked raisins to ours. We know many of you are used to cream cheese frosting on carrot cake. At the bakery, we use cream cheese frosting on the outside, but we like to slather white chocolate frosting between the layers. Feel free to use cream cheese frosting on the inside as well, if you prefer. To top things off, we cover the sides with toasted pecans. The result is a moist, flavorful, eye-catching dessert that's suitable for both special days and every day.

Serves: 20 people

---

1 In a medium bowl, combine the raisins with ½ cup boiling water and pineapple rum. Soak until the raisins are plump, about 1 hour.

2 Preheat the oven to 350°F. Coat three 9-inch round cake pans with the room temperature butter.

3 In a small bowl, combine the carrots and lemon juice.

Active time:
30 minutes

Total time:
1 hour and 20 minutes

- 1 cup dark raisins
- ½ cup boiling water
- 2 teaspoons pineapple rum
- 1 tablespoon unsalted butter, at room temperature, plus 2½ sticks (1¼ cups) unsalted butter, melted
- 8 medium carrots, peeled and finely shredded (2 cups packed)
- ¼ cup fresh lemon juice
- 1¾ cups all-purpose flour
- 1¾ cups cake flour
- 2 teaspoons baking soda
- 1 teaspoon baking powder
- ¾ teaspoon ground cinnamon
- ¼ teaspoon ground nutmeg
- ¾ teaspoon regular salt
- 5 large eggs
- 1½ cups granulated sugar

1 cup packed light brown sugar

1 ½ teaspoons pure vanilla extract

1 tablespoon vegetable oil

1 cup buttermilk

1 recipe White Chocolate Buttercream (recipe follows)

1 recipe (2 cups) Cream Cheese Frosting (see page 65)

2½ cups roasted pecans, for garnish (optional; see page 84)

4 In another medium bowl, whisk together the all-purpose flour, cake flour, baking soda, baking powder, cinnamon, nutmeg, and salt.

5 In the bowl of a stand mixer fitted with the paddle attachment, beat the eggs on medium speed until blended. Add the granulated sugar, brown sugar, and vanilla and beat until smooth, scraping the bowl as necessary, about 2 minutes.

6 Add the melted butter, vegetable oil, and buttermilk to the egg mixture and beat until blended, about 2 minutes. Reduce the mixer speed to low and gradually add the flour mixture, beating until blended. Drain the liquid from the carrots and the raisins. Using a wooden spoon, stir the carrots and raisins into the batter.

7 Divide the batter equally among the prepared pans and bake until a wooden pick inserted into the center comes out clean, 26 to 28 minutes. Let the cakes cool in the pans for 10 minutes before turning them out onto a wire rack to cool completely.

8 To assemble and frost the cakes, place 1 cake layer, bottom-side up, on a cake plate. Use an offset spatula to spread 1 cup of the White Chocolate Buttercream on top. Add the second cake layer, bottom-side down, and spread 1 cup of the buttercream on top. Top with the third cake layer, bottom-side up. Frost the top and sides of the cake with the Cream Cheese Frosting. Use the palm of your hand to gently press the nuts onto the sides of the cake.

WHITE CHOCOLATE BUTTERCREAM

Makes: 2½ cups

Active time:
30 minutes

Total time:
45 minutes

1 Combine the white chocolate and butter in a microwave-safe bowl and microwave until they are melted, stirring every 15 to 20 seconds.

2 In the bowl of a stand mixer fitted with the paddle attachment, mix the cream cheese, vanilla, and salt together on high speed until smooth, 1 to 2 minutes.

3 Reduce the mixer speed to low. Add the melted white chocolate mixture and beat for about 30 seconds. Scrape the bowl. Gradually add the confectioners' sugar and beat until blended. Scrape the bowl again. Increase the mixer speed to high and beat for 1 minute. Set aside until ready to use.

6 ounces white chocolate, chopped

2 tablespoons unsalted butter

One 8-ounce package Philadelphia® cream cheese, at room temperature

1 teaspoon pure vanilla extract

Pinch of regular salt

12 ounces (3 cups) confectioners' sugar

EVA

GRANDMOM WAS FIFTEEN YEARS old when the grandmother who raised her, Eliza, passed away, and Grandmom moved from Virginia back to Philadelphia to live with her mother's brother, Uncle Tommy, and his wife, Aunt Eva.

From the outside, Uncle Tommy and Aunt Eva were somewhat mismatched. He was a fair-skinned man; she was a dark-skinned woman. At that time, in their community, that was an uncommon combination because skin color affected your social caste, and men usually chose to marry up, which meant marrying lighter-skinned women. But Aunt Eva was a cute little lady, small and curvy and dainty, who wore corsets with the string in the back and hats and gloves when she traveled. She was attractive, savvy, and hardworking, and Uncle Tommy just adored her.

Still, there were plenty of women always trying to figure out what Uncle Tommy saw in Aunt Eva and whether they could get in between the two, or at least that's what Aunt Eva thought. Every Sunday, she'd instruct Grandmom, "As soon as church is over, you go right downstairs to the car, and sit in the middle seat right until I come out." This, of course, would prevent the church women interested in Uncle Tommy from trying to talk him up as he waited for Aunt Eva to get down from the choir loft. Grandmom, who had been taught to respect her elders, would reply, "Yes, ma'am," and did as told. Every time. Surely, Uncle Tommy knew what the two of them were up to, but he never let on.

Grandmom adored Aunt Eva just as much as Uncle Tommy did. Aunt Eva was everything Grandmom wanted to be: confident, opinionated, charismatic, and smart. She was smart enough to figure out a way to manipulate Grandmom's birth certificate so she would be eligible for high school even though she was already past the age for entry. Aunt Eva knew that education would make the difference between Betty finding a good job and living a comfortable life or not. As usual, she was right.

And it was Aunt Eva who introduced Betty to her husband, Leon Paul Hinton. Aunt Eva had known Leon from Pinn Memorial Baptist Church. She and some of the other elder women from church would write to the young men fighting in World War II, including Leon, to keep them encouraged. In turn, Leon would write Aunt Eva letters back to tell her what it was like in the various countries where he was stationed. Those letters impressed Aunt Eva so much that she advised Grandmom to marry Leon when he returned before someone else "snatched him up." Sure enough, when Leon got back from the war, he and Betty began a courtship that led to a fifty-five-year marriage.

Decades later, by the time I had come along, my grandmom and her brothers were still telling stories about Aunt Eva, like how she liked to say it wasn't "ladylike" for women to eat in front of others. Grandmom says Aunt Eva never ate dinner—she would say, "I'm not hungry," having already eaten in the kitchen. To this day, Grandmom will sit at the dinner table, let everyone fill their plates, and then eat small portions, even if she goes back for more later.

We named this cake "Aunt Eva Says" because Grandmom faithfully did everything "Aunt Eva said," and also because, well . . . Aunt Eva probably would have told us to.

AUNT EVA SAYS

Pineapple Pound Cake

When I was little, I used to love pineapple upside-down cake. What child can say no to cake topped with pineapple and maraschino cherries and slathered with caramelized brown sugar? And while upside-down cakes might be thought of as a bit commonplace these days, I still enjoy that combination of flavors. So we remixed an old-school recipe here and dressed it in a more sophisticated package.

Serves: 20 people

---

1 Preheat the oven to 350°F. Line two 9-inch round cake pans with parchment paper and coat lightly with nonstick cooking spray.

2 In a medium bowl, whisk together the flour, baking powder, and salt.

3 In the bowl of a stand mixer fitted with the paddle attachment, beat the butter until light and fluffy and then add the sugar on low speed until smooth, about 2 minutes. Add the eggs and egg yolks, 1 at a time, beating to blend and scraping the bowl as necessary. Add the crushed pineapple, vanilla, and pineapple rum and mix on medium speed until blended.

Active time:
35 minutes

Total time:
1 hour and 10 minutes

Nonstick cooking spray with flour

3 cups all-purpose flour

1¾ teaspoons baking powder

1 teaspoon regular salt

3 sticks (1½ cups) unsalted butter, at room temperature

2½ cups granulated sugar

5 large eggs, at room temperature

3 large egg yolks, at room temperature

1 cup crushed pineapple, drained

1 teaspoon pure vanilla extract

2 teaspoons pineapple rum

¼ cup whole milk

1 recipe Cream Cheese Frosting (recipe follows)

4 Reduce the mixer speed to low and alternately add
   the flour mixture and the milk to the butter mixture,
   beginning and ending with the flour mixture and
   mixing until well incorporated.

5 Divide the batter equally between the prepared pans
   and bake until a wooden pick inserted into the center
   comes out clean, 30 to 35 minutes. Let the cakes
   cool in the pans for 10 minutes before turning them
   out onto a wire rack to cool completely. Remove the
   parchment paper from the cakes.

6 To assemble and frost the cakes, place 1 cake layer,
   bottom-side up, on a cake plate. Use an offset spatula
   to spread 1 cup of the frosting on top. Add the second
   cake layer, bottom-side up. Frost the top and sides of
   the cake with the remaining frosting.

CREAM CHEESE FROSTING

Active time:
10 minutes

Total time:
18 minutes

Makes: 3 cups

1 In the bowl of a stand mixer fitted with the paddle attachment, beat the cream cheese and vanilla together on high speed until light and creamy, about 3 minutes. Reduce the mixer speed to medium. Add the butter and beat, scraping the bowl as necessary, until blended.

2 Reduce the mixer speed to low and gradually add the confectioners' sugar, beating until blended. Increase the mixer speed to high and beat until light and fluffy, about 1 minute. Mix in a drop or two of yellow food coloring, if desired. Set aside until ready to use.

One 8-ounce package Philadelphia® cream cheese, at room temperature

1 teaspoon pure vanilla extract

1 stick (8 tablespoons) unsalted butter, at room temperature

1 pound confectioners' sugar

Yellow food coloring (optional)

COMPANY'S COMIN'

Coconut Cake

The bakery's first ever review, in *Philadelphia Weekly*, was of this dense, but extremely moist, three-layer coconut cake. My childhood friend, Khalilah, had to read the review to me, because I was too nervous to do it myself, and when I heard the cake being described as a "three-layer extravaganza," I knew we had knocked it out of the park. To think, we had debated whether or not to even make coconut cake for that review, because so many people say they don't like it. I've since learned those folks haven't had good coconut cake. Our coconut cake.

Serves: 20 (or more) people

1 Preheat the oven to 350°F. Coat three 9-inch round cake pans with vegetable shortening, line the bottoms of the pans with parchment paper, and spray with nonstick cooking spray.

2 In a large bowl, whisk together the flour, baking powder, and salt.

3 In the bowl of a stand mixer fitted with the paddle attachment, beat the butter until light and fluffy and then add the sugar on low speed until smooth, about 3 minutes. Add the eggs and egg yolks, 1 at a time, beating until blended and scraping the bowl as necessary.

Active time:
25 minutes

Total time:
60 minutes

Vegetable shortening

Nonstick cooking spray with flour

3½ cups all-purpose flour

1¼ teaspoons baking powder

½ teaspoon regular salt

3 sticks (1½ cups) unsalted butter, at room temperature

2¼ cups plus 2 tablespoons granulated sugar

5 large eggs

2 large egg yolks

1 cup heavy cream

⅓ cup evaporated milk

1 tablespoon pure vanilla extract

1 recipe Company's Comin' Filling (recipe follows)

1 recipe Company's Comin' Cream Cheese Frosting (see page 71)

4 cups sweetened flaked coconut

4 Reduce the mixer speed to low. Add the cream, milk, and vanilla and beat until smooth. Add the flour mixture and beat until blended. Increase the mixer speed to high and beat until smooth, about 1 minute.

5 Divide the batter equally among the prepared pans. Bake until a wooden pick inserted into the center comes out clean, 30 to 35 minutes. Let the cakes cool in the pans for 10 minutes before turning them out onto wire racks to cool completely. Remove the parchment paper.

6 To assemble and frost the cakes, place 1 cake layer, bottom-side up, on a cake plate. Use an offset spatula to spread half of the filling on top. Add the second cake layer, bottom-side down, and spread with the remaining filling. Top with the third layer, bottom-side up. Use a large offset spatula to spread the frosting over the top and sides of the cake. Use the palm of your hand to gently press the coconut onto the sides and top of the cake.

Company's Comin' Filling

Makes: 2 cups

1 In a small bowl, stir the cornstarch, 2 tablespoons water, and vanilla until the cornstarch has dissolved.

2 In a medium saucepan over medium heat, stir the cream, milk, sugar, and butter until melted and smooth. Add the cornstarch mixture to the cream mixture and bring to a boil. Remove from the heat and stir in the coconut. Cool to room temperature.

3 Stir the sour cream into the cooled coconut mixture. Cover and refrigerate for 4 hours or overnight.

Active time:
20 minutes

Total time:
20 minutes

2 tablespoons cornstarch

2 tablespoons water

1½ teaspoons pure vanilla extract

1 cup heavy cream

¼ cup evaporated milk

½ cup granulated sugar

1 stick (8 tablespoons) unsalted butter

2¼ cups sweetened flaked coconut

¼ cup sour cream

Company's Comin' Cream Cheese Frosting

Makes: 3 cups

1 In the bowl of a stand mixer fitted with the paddle attachment, beat the cream cheese on medium speed until light and fluffy, about 3 minutes. Add the butter and beat until fluffy, scraping the bowl as necessary, about 3 minutes.

2 Reduce the mixer speed to low and beat in the confectioner's sugar and vanilla until blended, scraping the bowl as necessary. Increase the mixer speed to high and beat until fluffy. Set aside until ready to use.

Active time:
10 minutes

Total time:
20 minutes

- Two 8-ounce packages Philadelphia® cream cheese, at room temperature
- 1 stick (8 tablespoons) unsalted butter, at room temperature
- 2 cups confectioners' sugar
- 1½ teaspoons pure vanilla extract

SING LITTLE ALICE

Marble Pound Cake

There was a time in Philadelphia, not too long ago, that every wedding cake vendor was pushing chocolate chip cake. I get why—a hint of chocolate within a vanilla cake is appealing—but I just don't think chocolate chips are the best way to achieve that result. We attempted to find a balance by creating this vanilla and chocolate swirl cake. It takes a bit of work, because it requires making two cake batters and then swirling them together, but it's worth the extra effort.

Serves: 15 to 20 people

1 Preheat the oven to 350°F. Coat three 9-inch round cake pans with vegetable shortening, line the bottoms with parchment paper, and spray with nonstick cooking spray.

2 Make the vanilla batter first. In a medium bowl, whisk together the flour, salt, baking powder, and baking soda.

3 In the bowl of a stand mixer fitted with the paddle attachment, beat the butter and sugar on medium speed until light and fluffy, scraping the bowl as necessary, about 3 minutes. Add the eggs, 1 at a time, beating until blended and scraping the bowl as necessary. Add the vanilla and rum extracts and beat until blended.

Active time:
60 minutes

Total time:
1 hour and 30 minutes

Vegetable shortening

Nonstick cooking spray with flour

VANILLA BATTER

4 cups cake flour

¾ teaspoon regular salt

½ teaspoon baking powder

¼ teaspoon baking soda

3 sticks (1½ cups) unsalted butter, at room temperature

3 cups granulated sugar

8 large eggs

1½ teaspoons pure vanilla extract

¼ teaspoon pure rum extract

1 cup sour cream

continued on the following page

4 Reduce the mixer speed to low and alternately add the flour mixture and sour cream to the butter mixture, beginning and ending with the flour mixture and beating until smooth.

5 Now make the chocolate batter. In a large bowl, whisk together the cocoa powder, sour cream, eggs, egg yolks, and vanilla until smooth.

6 In the bowl of a stand mixer fitted with the paddle attachment, beat the flour, baking powder, baking soda, salt, and sugar on low speed just until blended. Add the butter and half of the cocoa mixture and beat on low speed until the dry ingredients are just moist. Increase the mixer speed to medium and beat until blended, scraping the bowl as necessary, 1 to 2 minutes.

7 Gradually add the remaining cocoa mixture in 2 batches, beating 20 seconds after each addition. Add ½ cup boiling water and beat until smooth.

8 Pour 2 cups of vanilla batter and 1 cup of chocolate batter into each prepared pan and swirl together with a butter knife. Be careful not to stir the batter. Bake until a wooden pick inserted into the center comes out clean, 25 to 30 minutes. Let the cakes cool in the pans for 10 minutes before turning them out onto a wire rack to cool completely. Remove the parchment paper.

continued from page 73

CHOCOLATE BATTER

½ cup plus 3 tablespoons unsweetened Dutch-process cocoa powder

¾ cup sour cream

2 large eggs

2 large egg yolks

1½ teaspoons pure vanilla extract

2¼ cups cake flour

1 teaspoon baking powder

½ teaspoon baking soda

¾ teaspoon regular salt

1¾ cups granulated sugar

2 sticks (1 cup) unsalted butter, at room temperature

½ cup boiling water

1 recipe Vanilla Buttercream (see page 22)

3 cups Chocolate Buttercream (see page 91)

9 To assemble and frost the cakes, place 1 cake layer, bottom-side up, on a cake plate. Use an offset spatula to swirl ½ cup Vanilla Buttercream and ½ cup Chocolate Buttercream on top. Add the second layer, bottom-side down, and swirl ½ cup of each buttercream on top. Top with the third cake layer, bottom-side up. Swirl the remaining buttercreams on the top and sides of the cake.

JEAN'S ROAD TRIP

Red Velvet Cake with Cream Cheese Frosting

Some things are just meant to be. And so it was for red velvet cake and Brown Betty. How else could we explain how a cake we didn't grow up eating—and had never made before—became our number one seller? One of our first brides asked us to develop a red velvet batter for her groom's cake "because he was from the South and it was his favorite." Three tries later, and viola! Deep red, moist chocolate, cream cheese–topped deliciousness emerged. We decided to try it out on the cupcake menu just for some variety, but when one of the food writers at the *Philadelphia Inquirer* did a three-page story on it, the rest was history, and we cannot keep enough in the store.

Serves: 20 people

---

1. Preheat the oven to 350°F. Coat three 9-inch round cake pans with vegetable shortening, line the bottoms of the pans with parchment paper, and spray with nonstick cooking spray.

2. In the bowl of a stand mixer fitted with the paddle attachment, beat the flour, sugar, cocoa powder, baking powder, baking soda, and salt on low speed to blend.

Active time:
30 minutes

Total time:
60 minutes

Vegetable shortening

Nonstick cooking spray with flour

2¼ cups all-purpose flour

2 cups granulated sugar

½ cup plus 3 tablespoons unsweetened Dutch-process cocoa powder

¾ teaspoon baking powder

¾ teaspoon baking soda

¾ teaspoon regular salt

¾ cup buttermilk

2 sticks (1 cup) unsalted butter, melted

2 large eggs

2 large egg yolks

1½ teaspoons pure vanilla extract

1 tablespoon red food coloring (½ ounce)

¾ cup boiling water

1 recipe Cream Cheese Buttercream (see page 120)

3 In a large bowl, mix the buttermilk, butter, eggs, egg yolks, vanilla, and food coloring until just blended.

4 Add the buttermilk mixture to the flour mixture in 2 batches, beating on low speed until blended. Increase the mixer speed to high and beat until smooth. Reduce the mixer speed to low, slowly pour in ¾ cup boiling water, and beat until blended. The batter will be thin.

5 Divide the batter equally among the prepared pans and bake until a wooden pick inserted into the center comes out clean, 25 to 30 minutes. Let the cakes cool in the pans for 15 minutes before turning them out onto wire racks to cool completely. Remove the parchment paper.

6 To assemble and frost the cakes, place 1 cake layer, bottom-side up, on a cake plate. Use an offset spatula to spread 1 cup of the buttercream on top. Add the second cake layer, bottom-side down, and spread 1 cup of the buttercream on top. Top with the third cake layer, bottom-side up. Frost the top and sides of the cake with the remaining buttercream.

ASK ROSE

Dutch Chocolate Cake with a Raspberry Filling and Chocolate Buttercream

Some flavors go together naturally. Peanut butter and jelly. Oatmeal and raisins. Chocolate and raspberries. That last combination describes our Ask Rose cake. It is a lovely, light chocolate cake with a sweet, but slightly tart raspberry puree filling - a match made in cake heaven.

Serves: 20 people

---

1 Preheat the oven to 350°F. Coat two 9-inch round cake pans with vegetable shortening, line the bottoms of the pans with parchment paper, and spray with nonstick cooking spray.

2 In a large bowl, mix the cocoa powder, sour cream, eggs, egg yolks, and vanilla until smooth.

3 In the bowl of a stand mixer fitted with the paddle attachment, beat the flour, baking powder, baking soda, salt, and sugar on low speed just until blended. Add the butter and half of the cocoa mixture and beat on low speed until the dry ingredients are just moist. Increase the mixer speed to medium and beat until blended, scraping the bowl as necessary, 1 to 2 minutes.

Active time:
30 minutes

Total time:
60 minutes

Vegetable shortening

Nonstick cooking spray with flour

½ cup plus 3 tablespoons unsweetened Dutch-process cocoa powder

¾ cup sour cream

2 large eggs

2 large egg yolks

1½ teaspoon pure vanilla extract

2¼ cups cake flour

1 teaspoon baking powder

½ teaspoon baking soda

¾ teaspoon regular salt

1¾ cups granulated sugar

2 sticks (1 cup) unsalted butter, at room temperature

½ cup boiling water

1 recipe Raspberry Filling (recipe follows)

1 recipe Chocolate Buttercream (see page 91)

4 Gradually add the remaining cocoa mixture in
   2 batches, beating 20 seconds after each addition.
   Add ½ cup boiling water and beat until smooth.

5 Divide the batter equally among the prepared pans
   and smooth the top with an offset spatula. Bake until
   a wooden pick inserted into the center comes out
   clean, 25 to 30 minutes. Let the cakes cool in the
   pans for 10 minutes before turning them out onto a
   wire rack to cool completely. Remove the parchment
   paper.

6 To assemble and frost the cakes, place 1 cake layer,
   bottom-side up, on a cake plate. Use an offset spatula
   to spread the Raspberry Filling on top. Place the
   second cake layer, bottom-side up, on top. Frost the
   top and sides of the cake with the buttercream.

Raspberry Filling

Makes: 1 cup

1 Using a food processor, pulse the raspberries until
   smooth. Strain the raspberries through a fine-mesh
   strainer.

2 In a medium saucepan over medium heat, stir the
   strained raspberries, jelly, and cornstarch. Cook,
   stirring occasionally, until the mixture bubbles and
   thickens slightly. Transfer to a medium bowl and let
   cool to room temperature.

Active time:
20 minutes

Total time:
20 minutes

10 ounces frozen
raspberries, thawed

½ cup currant jelly

1 tablespoon plus 2
teaspoons cornstarch

HEY THELMA

Chocolate Buttermilk Cake with Caramel Coconut Filling

I must confess: I am not a fan of chocolate. In fact, I really don't eat it at all. But this cake is one of those exceptions. The caramel filling in between each spongy layer of buttermilk chocolate cake is just too good, and with the chocolate cognac glaze, it makes a stunning presentation.

Serves: 20 people

---

1 Preheat the oven to 350°F. Coat two 9-inch round cake pans with vegetable shortening, line the bottoms of the pans with parchment paper, and spray the pans with nonstick cooking spray.

2 In the bowl of a stand mixer fitted with the paddle attachment, mix the flour, sugar, cocoa powder, baking powder, baking soda, and salt on low speed.

3 In a large bowl, mix together the buttermilk, butter, eggs, egg yolks, and vanilla until just blended.

4 Add the buttermilk mixture to the flour mixture in 2 batches, beating on low speed until blended. Increase the mixer speed to high and beat until smooth. Reduce the mixer speed to low and slowly pour in ¾ cup boiling water, beating until blended. The batter will be thin.

Active time:
25 minutes

Total time:
55 minutes

Vegetable shortening

Nonstick cooking spray with flour

2¼ cups all-purpose flour

2 cups granulated sugar

½ cup plus 3 tablespoons unsweetened Dutch-process cocoa powder

¾ teaspoon baking powder

¾ teaspoon baking soda

¾ teaspoon regular salt

¾ cup buttermilk

2 sticks (1 cup) unsalted butter, melted

2 large eggs

2 large egg yolks

1½ teaspoons pure vanilla extract

¾ cup boiling water

1 recipe Caramel Coconut Filling (recipe follows)

1 recipe Chocolate Glaze (see page 85)

5 Divide the batter equally between the prepared pans and bake until a wooden pick inserted into the center comes out clean, about 28 minutes. Let the cakes cool in the pans for 15 minutes before turning them out onto wire racks to cool completely.

6 To assemble and glaze the cakes, place 1 cake layer, bottom-side up, on a cake plate. Use an offset spatula to spread the filling on top. Add the second cake layer, bottom-side up. Pour 1 cup of the glaze over the center of the top of the cake and use an offset spatula to spread the glaze over the top and sides of the cake. Chill the cake until the glaze is set, about 15 minutes.

7 Pour the remaining glaze over the cake and spread it, covering the top and sides of the cake. Chill until the glaze is set, about 3 hours.

Caramel Coconut Filling

Makes: 1½ cups

1 Arrange the oven racks in the upper and lower thirds of the oven. Preheat the oven to 325°F.

2 Spread the coconut and pecans on 2 separate rimmed baking sheets. Place the pecans on the upper rack of the oven, and the coconut on the lower rack of the oven. Bake the nuts and coconut until golden, stirring occasionally, 10 to 16 minutes. Set aside to cool to room temperature.

Active time:
10 minutes

Total time:
1 hour and 56 minutes

1 cup sweetened flaked coconut

¾ cup chopped pecans

One 14-ounce can sweetened condensed milk

1 tablespoon pure vanilla extract

3 Increase the oven temperature to 425°F. Pour the condensed milk into a 9-inch pie pan. Cover tightly with foil. Place the pie pan in a large roasting pan, fill the roasting pan halfway with boiling water, and bake for 45 minutes. Refill the roasting pan with water, if necessary, and continue to bake the condensed milk until it is caramel colored and thick, about 35 minutes longer. Remove the pie pan from the oven and stir the coconut, pecans, and vanilla into the thickened condensed milk. Cover with foil to keep warm until ready to use.

Chocolate Glaze

Makes: 2 cups

1 In a bowl set over a medium saucepan of simmering water, stir together the chocolate, butter, and corn syrup until melted and smooth, about 5 minutes. Remove from the heat. Add the cognac and stir to blend.

2 Let the glaze cool until lukewarm but still pourable, stirring occasionally, about 20 minutes. Set aside until ready to use.

Active time:
15 minutes

Total time:
45 minutes

10 ounces semisweet chocolate, chopped

2½ sticks (1¼ cups) unsalted butter

3 tablespoons light corn syrup

1 tablespoon cognac

HATTIE

Grandmom's mother-in-law, Hattie Hinton, was fierce and put a bit of fear in everyone's heart. Never the type to hold her tongue, Hattie would tell you how it was—if you were wrong or she didn't like what you were up to, she let you know it. And she always did it with a healthy helping of the good Lord in her heart, saying things like, "God doesn't like this now," or "The good Lord doesn't like you to do that," to emphasize her point.

My grandmom tells the story of when she was a new wife and how Hattie was all over her to make sure she did everything just right for my grandpop. It was a little intimidating for his new bride because, knowing Hattie was a sharp-tongued woman, Grandmom didn't want to get on her bad side. No one did.

Hattie was all about manners and respect. She read her Bible every day, always had it within reach and beside her bed, and often quoted from it, teaching the children in the family about the scripture and what it meant. Every Sunday after church (she never missed a service), Hattie served a feast—cakes, pies, three to four different meats and veggies—and she would talk about the day's sermon. Cousin Felice, whom we all called "Cousin Fee," remembers Hattie teaching her many of the Old Testament stories. "She told me that one day blood would run in the street as high as a horse's hoof," Cousin Fee has said. "I didn't know what a horse's hoof was, but I didn't dare ask her. I just remember going to the front door and looking outside for the blood."

Hattie was a fine, upstanding woman who walked proudly, carrying herself like a lady. She used to say that's what a woman was supposed to do—walk with her head held up high. And even though she was a short and somewhat stout woman, Hattie earned the respect of those around her.

But underneath that tough exterior, Hattie had a heart of gold. She loved children and often babysat my mom, my cousins, and some of the kids who lived on her block while their parents worked. Hattie's home wasn't too far from Lancaster Avenue, one of the main shopping centers of town, where there was an A&P store, one of the largest supermarkets in Philadelphia. Virtually everyone in the neighborhood went shopping there, and many women would walk past Hattie's house on their way back home, hauling groceries and shopping bags, and Hattie would always let them use her bathroom. She'd say, "Sweetheart, do you have to go to the ladies' room? Well, just leave your bags here on the porch, and go right inside."

Even with all those children and all that traffic, Hattie's home was immaculate. She was a very clean woman. At the time, there was no such thing as a mop—you had to get on your hands and knees to scrub the floor, and that's just what Hattie did. She got right down and scrubbed the floors, the steps, and the front porch. If it's true that cleanliness is next to godliness, then Hattie was as close to God as they come.

To honor Hattie—a multifaceted woman who liked to speak her mind and open her heart—we've dedicated our triple-layer chocolate ganache cake. We figured it was either that or a real tough cookie.

HATTIE DON'T PLAY

Chocolate Ganache Layer Cake

My mom, unlike me, loves chocolate. And before we opened the bakery, we would search far and wide for the most chocolaty cake we could find for her birthday every year. I have flown cake from California, driven cake from Brooklyn, and ordered cake from South Carolina—all in an attempt to satisfy my mom's chocolate sweet tooth. Truth be told, she was never quite impressed. Naturally, achieving a true chocolate lover's dream cake was high on my mom's list of priorities when we were forming the menu, and we think this dark chocolate cake, with chocolate buttercream and chocolate ganache, came out even better than we had dreamed.

Serves: 20 people

1 Preheat the oven to 350°F. Line three 9-inch round cake pans with parchment paper and coat with nonstick cooking spray.

2 In a medium bowl, whisk together the cocoa powder and 1 cup boiling water until smooth. Cool to room temperature.

3 Meanwhile, in another medium bowl, mix one-fourth of the cocoa mixture with the eggs, egg yolks, buttermilk, and vanilla until blended.

Active time:
35 minutes

Total time:
1 hour and 10 minutes

Nonstick cooking spray with flour

1 cup plus 1 tablespoon unsweetened Dutch-process cocoa powder

1 cup boiling water

4 large eggs, at room temperature

4 large egg yolks, at room temperature

¼ cup buttermilk

2½ teaspoons pure vanilla extract

3½ cups cake flour

2¾ cups superfine sugar

2¼ teaspoons baking powder

¾ teaspoon regular salt

3 sticks (1½ cups) unsalted butter, at room temperature

1 recipe Chocolate Buttercream (recipe follows)

1 recipe Ganache (see page 92)

4   In the bowl of a stand mixer fitted with the paddle attachment, beat the flour, sugar, baking powder, and salt on low speed until blended. Add the butter and remaining three-fourths of the cocoa mixture and mix until the dry ingredients are moist, scraping the bowl as necessary, about 1 minute. Gradually add the egg mixture and mix until blended.

5   Divide the batter equally among the prepared pans. Use a small offset spatula to smooth the top of the batter. Bake until a wooden pick inserted into the center comes out almost clean, 30 to 35 minutes. Let the cakes cool in the pans for 10 minutes before turning them out onto a wire rack to cool completely. Remove the parchment paper.

6   To assemble and frost the cakes, place 1 cake layer, bottom-side up, on a cake plate. Use an offset spatula to spread 1 cup of the buttercream on top. Add the second cake layer, bottom-side down, and spread 1 cup of the buttercream on top. Top with the third cake layer, bottom-side up. Spread the remaining buttercream over the top and sides of the cake. Then spread the ganache over the top of the cake, allowing it to drip down the sides.

CHOCOLATE BUTTERCREAM

Makes: 3 cups

Active time:
12 minutes

Total time:
20 minutes

1 In the bowl of a stand mixer fitted with the paddle attachment, beat the cream cheese and vanilla together on low speed until smooth. Increase the mixer speed to high. Add the butter and beat until incorporated, scraping the bowl as necessary, about 1 minute.

2 Reduce the mixer speed to low and beat in the cocoa powder and corn syrup. Add the confectioners' sugar and beat until blended. Add the milk, 1 tablespoon at a time, beating until the buttercream achieves a spreadable consistency. Set aside until ready to use.

- 3 ounces Philadelphia® cream cheese, at room temperature
- 2 teaspoons pure vanilla extract
- 1 stick (8 tablespoons) unsalted butter, at room temperature
- ½ cup unsweetened dark cocoa powder
- 2 teaspoons light corn syrup
- 3½ cups confectioners' sugar
- 1 to 3 tablespoons whole milk

GANACHE

1 In a bowl set over a medium saucepan of simmering water, stir the chocolate until smooth and melted. Alternatively, in a medium microwave-safe bowl, microwave the chocolate on high in 15-second intervals, stirring occasionally, until smooth.

2 In a medium saucepan over medium heat, combine the cream and corn syrup and cook, stirring occasionally, just to the point of boiling. Remove from the heat.

3 Pour the cream mixture into the melted chocolate, stirring until blended. Stir in the cognac. Let cool to room temperature, about 2 hours. The ganache will thicken as it cools.

Active time:
15 minutes

Total time:
2 hours and 15 minutes

- 12 ounces bittersweet chocolate, chopped
- 1½ cups heavy cream
- 3 tablespoons light corn syrup
- 2 tablespoons cognac or your favorite liqueur

WITH CHERRIES ON TOP CHEESECAKE

Long before we ever thought of opening a bakery, my mom was receiving "orders" for this cheesecake for graduations, birthdays, and holidays. Its creamy texture coupled with a buttery and crisp graham cracker crust provide a singularly rich taste. To top it off, we soak whole dark cherries in cordial overnight before making the sauce. Keep in mind that this one takes time to make, but, trust us, your guests will wait.

Serves: 12 to 14 people

1 Preheat the oven to 425°F. Place a baking sheet on the bottom rack of the oven to catch any drippings. Coat the bottom and sides of a 9-inch springform pan with shortening.

2 In a medium bowl, mix the crumbs, butter, and 2 tablespoons of the sugar until well blended. Press the crumb mixture onto the bottom and sides of the prepared pan, stopping 2 inches from the top. Refrigerate the crust while preparing the filling.

3 In the bowl of a stand mixer fitted with the paddle attachment, beat the cream cheese on medium speed until light and fluffy. Add the remaining 1 cup of sugar and beat on medium speed until smooth and light. Scrape the bowl. Reduce the mixer speed to

Active time:
40 minutes

Total time:
2 hours and 20 minutes, plus at least 2 hours of refrigeration time

Vegetable shortening

1½ cups graham cracker crumbs

1 stick (8 tablespoons) unsalted butter, melted

2 tablespoons plus 1 cup granulated sugar

Four 8-ounce packages Philadelphia® cream cheese, at room temperature

2 large eggs, lightly beaten

2 tablespoons cornstarch

1 teaspoon pure vanilla extract

¾ cup sour cream

1 recipe Dark Cherry Topping (recipe follows)

low and beat in the eggs, cornstarch, and vanilla until just blended. Mix in the sour cream until just blended, about 30 seconds.

4 Pour the mixture into the crust in the springform pan and bake 10 minutes. Reduce the oven temperature to 270°F and bake until the filling is set, about 45 minutes longer. Turn off the oven, open the door slightly, and let the cake cool for 45 minutes to 1 hour.

5 Remove the cake from the oven and set it on a wire rack. Let it continue to cool for a couple of hours. Remove the pan sides from the cake and refrigerate the cake for at least 2 hours or overnight.

6 To serve, remove the cheesecake from the bottom of the pan and top with the Dark Cherry Topping.

DARK CHERRY TOPPING

Makes: 1½ cups

1   Place the cherries in a colander set over a bowl to defrost, at least 1 hour. Add enough water to the strained juice in the bowl to equal 1 cup.

2   In a medium saucepan, stir the 1 cup of juice, cherry wine, sugar, and corn syrup over medium heat until the sugar dissolves. Add the cherries and bring to a boil. Cover and refrigerate overnight.

3   The next day, place the cherries in a colander set over a medium microwave-safe bowl to drain. Microwave the bowl of cherry juice on high in 30-second increments until reduced to ¾ cup. Let cool completely.

4   In a medium saucepan, whisk together the cornstarch, tapioca, and salt. Gradually stir in the cooled cherry liquid, bring it to a boil, and continue to cook until the sauce thickens. The mixture should barely drop from the spoon. Add the cherries and simmer until heated through, about 1 minute. Remove from the heat and stir in the almond extract.

5   Let the sauce cool before spooning it over the cold cheesecake. The sauce can be kept in an airtight container in the refrigerator for up to 1 month.

Active time:
30 minutes

Total time:
1 hour and 30 minutes,
plus overnight
refrigeration time

One 16-ounce bag frozen dark pitted cherries (without added sugar)

6 tablespoons cherry wine, such as Kijafa

5 tablespoons granulated sugar

1 teaspoon light corn syrup

1 tablespoon plus ½ teaspoon cornstarch

1 tablespoon tapioca

Pinch of regular salt

⅛ teaspoon pure almond extract

MARY

MARY EVANS WAS GRANDMOM'S maternal aunt. Everyone in the family called her "Aunt Bunch"; Bunch was just her nickname. She and Grandmom's mother, Ruth, had married the Gaskins brothers of Philadelphia. As the story goes, their mother had warned them: "Two sisters marrying two brothers is never going to work." And it didn't. Aunt Bunch eventually left her husband—"too much of a ladies' man," she said (all five Gaskins brothers apparently "had a problem" with the ladies). Aunt Bunch never remarried nor had any children. She used to say that one husband was enough. Instead, she loved Grandmom and her two brothers as if they were her own.

Tall and slim with very fair skin, Aunt Bunch had beautifully thick, black hair that she never "wore out" or let hang down her back. She was much too humble, Grandmom said, so she pinned it up in a big knot, like a bun. But Aunt Bunch was always interested in hair, in what it could do and how it behaved. After she split from her husband, she worked at a dry cleaners until she signed up to attend a special program created by the NAACP to help black women enroll—and be accepted into—beauty school. Although Aunt Bunch was older, probably in her late thirties, than most of the girls attending the school, she thought it was a good opportunity since she had to support herself now. She graduated at the top of her class.

Aunt Bunch worked out of her home for a few years, built a strong clientele, and eventually saved enough money to open her own salon, Mary's Beauty Shop, in West Philadelphia on the corner of 48th Street and Fairmount Avenue. Business became so good that she eventually bought the entire building, conveniently living right upstairs on the second floor.

Mary's Beauty Shop was a success from the start. Everyone in the neighborhood went there. People used to say that "whatever she uses on the hair makes the curl last," and on any day of the week that beauty parlor was filled with the smoke of the straightening comb, and with women laughing and gossiping. Grandmom worked there after school as a shampoo girl. Aunt Bunch taught Grandmom how to work up a good lather and give the ladies a nice scalp massage at the same time. My grandmom was a quick study, and soon she became the most sought after shampoo girl in the shop.

Aunt Bunch was very good to us—she watched my mom every day while my grandmom and grandpop worked; she walked her to school and made her breakfast and lunch. When I was a little girl, Aunt Bunch often babysat me too, and I used to play in the shop—digging through old things and pretending that I was doing hair. Grandmom, out of appreciation, took care of Aunt Bunch later in her life when she became sick and had to close the salon. After Aunt Bunch passed away, my grandmom and her brothers were left the building, and they leased it to a young hairdresser in the neighborhood, so a beauty shop is still there to this day.

We named the sweet potato cheesecake "To Miss Mary" as a reminder of how the beauty parlor customers and hairdressers would run Grandmom back and forth in the shop telling her to give this or that "to Miss Mary." Perhaps the only way to describe this wonderful cake, baked in a graham cracker crust and topped with a sour cream frosting, is to say it's bursting with flavor. Or that it's chock-full. Just like Grandmom's tip jar used to be.

TO MISS MARY

Sweet Potato Cheesecake

In 2004, when we opened the bakery, it seemed like every soul food restaurant had sweet potato cheesecake on the menu, so I felt pressured not only to put it on our menu, but to make it a standout. We did that by roasting whole sweet potatoes, mashing and straining them, and adding them to our batter—all that roasting, mashing, and straining takes time, but it's worth it to get that true and vibrant sweet potato flavor. Ever since, sweet potato cheesecake remains our most popular Thanksgiving dessert.

Serves: 12 to 14 people

---

1 To make the mashed sweet potatoes, preheat the oven to 350°F. Line a rimmed baking sheet with foil. Place the potatoes on the baking sheet and rub the skins with oil.

2 Roast the potatoes until tender when pierced with a fork, 50 to 55 minutes. Set the potatoes aside until they are cool enough to handle. Using a knife remove the skin of the sweet potatoes and place the flesh of the potatoes in the bowl of a stand mixer fitted with the paddle attachment. Beat the potato flesh on medium-high speed to remove the pulp, about 1 minute. Push the flesh through a fine-mesh strainer over a medium bowl. Set aside. Reduce the oven temperature to 175°F.

Active time:
45 minutes

Total time:
2 hours and 25 minutes, plus at least 2 hours of refrigeration time

MASHED SWEET POTATOES

- I pound sweet potatoes or yams, scrubbed
- I tablespoon vegetable oil

GRAHAM CRACKER CRUST

- Vegetable shortening
- 2 cups graham cracker crumbs
- I stick (8 tablespoons) unsalted butter, melted
- 2 tablespoons superfine sugar

CHEESECAKE FILLING

- Three 8-ounce packages Philadelphia® cream cheese, at room temperature
- I¼ cups packed dark brown sugar

continued on the following page

3 Increase the oven temperature to 440°F. Place a baking sheet on the bottom rack of the oven to catch any drippings. Lightly coat the bottom and sides of a 9-inch springform pan with shortening.

4 To prepare the crust, in a small bowl, use your fingers to mix the crumbs, butter, and superfine sugar until blended.

5 Firmly press the crumb mixture onto the bottom and 2inches up the sides of the prepared pan. Refrigerate the crust while preparing the filling.

6 To prepare the filling, in the bowl of a stand mixer fitted with the paddle attachment, beat the cream cheese on medium speed until light and fluffy. Add the brown sugar and beat on low speed until smooth. Scrape the bowl. Add the mashed sweet potatoes and beat on medium speed until blended. Add the eggs, flour, vanilla, cinnamon, and nutmeg and beat until well blended.

7 Pour the batter into the crust and bake 10 minutes. Reduce the oven temperature to 250°F and bake until the filling is set, 80 to 85 minutes longer.

8 Meanwhile, prepare the sour cream topping. In a small bowl, mix the sour cream, superfine sugar, and vanilla to blend. Cover and refrigerate until ready to use.

continued from page 101

4 large eggs, lightly beaten, at room temperature

2 tablespoons all-purpose flour

1 ½ teaspoons pure vanilla extract

½ teaspoon ground cinnamon

¼ teaspoon ground nutmeg

SOUR CREAM TOPPING

1 cup sour cream

3 tablespoons plus 1 teaspoon superfine sugar

½ teaspoon pure vanilla extract

9 Remove the cake from the oven. Immediately spread the sour cream topping quickly and evenly over the cake. Return the cake to the oven. Increase the oven temperature to 350°F and bake for an additional 5 to 7 minutes; do not let the topping brown.

10 Remove the cake from the oven and transfer it to a wire rack to cool completely. Remove the pan sides from the cake. Use a large cake spatula to remove the cake from the bottom of the springform pan and transfer it to a cake plate. Refrigerate the cake until serving.

DOT

EVERY PHOTOGRAPH THAT I'VE ever seen of Dot Summers, Grandmom's first cousin, maid of honor, and dear friend, has her husband, Bill Summers, right there beside her. They were inseparable.

They met in the 1940s. Uncle Bill, a slim, handsome, and very popular fellow with silky smooth brown skin, was tall at 6 feet 3 inches, while Aunt Dot was just over 5 feet, on her tiptoes. From all accounts, they fell madly in love. Bill was drawn to Aunt Dot's bright, sparkly eyes, which would light up whenever he walked into the room. Uncle Bill played the saxophone and piano part-time in the local clubs—he would also play piano and sing—and when Dot would go to see him, he would serenade her in the same soft voice he'd later use to serenade the two children they had together, Mary and Billy. Dot and Bill's courtship was short before they got married, after which Bill left to serve in the military during the Korean War, while Dot went to work at Universal Dental Company with my grandmom, "Little" Aunt Alice, and Wilthium, Uncle Junior's wife.

When their daughter, Mary, was born, Bill came home, and together he and Dot lived for twenty-five years in a home built on love and commitment—and lots of pampering. "Oh, my mother spoiled us!" Cousin Mary likes to say. "First thing in the morning, she'd bring my brother and me hot cocoa and toast in bed to wake us up—that's before we went down to breakfast and had our oatmeal and cereal."

Aunt Dot kept a warm, cozy home and often took care of extended family, caring for uncles and aunts whenever they got very sick. She sewed her children's clothing, dressing Cousin Mary in pretty little velvet dresses, and took care to make sure the house always looked "just so." Cousin Mary likes to tell the story of when she asked Aunt Dot if she could bring her sixth-grade teacher home for lunch. "She fixed the most beautiful table for Mrs. Alexander," Mary recalls. "She put out the lace tablecloth and her fine china and fixed a wonderful luncheon. I was so proud of my mom. That's my fondest memory." Apparently, it was Bill who taught Dot how to cook, and she quickly became practiced and skillful in the kitchen—her specialties were macaroni and cheese, dump cake, and pineapple upside-down cake.

Aunt Dot and Uncle Bill had a love and confidence in one another that most folks only dream of, and, as a result, Cousin Mary can hardly remember them ever arguing at all. "Only one time in my entire childhood do I recall them having any sort of squabble. I remember my mother was doing the dishes, and Daddy put his arms around her, and I had the feeling that they had had a tiff," Cousin Mary has said, "but then she smiled, and that was that."

Bill died of cancer at a very young age, forty-four years old, and although Dot, who lived to be eighty-two years old, later remarried, Bill was always her one true love. Throughout their lives, everyone always knew them as a pair, as "Dot and Bill," and today their remains are buried together at the Beverly National Cemetery in New Jersey.

Our "Dot's First Love" cheesecake, blended with pure chocolate and Godiva liqueur, pays homage to that look Aunt Dot got in her eyes at the mere mention of Uncle Bill. With this cake, we celebrate love. At first bite.

DOT'S FIRST LOVE

Chocolate Cheesecake

You've heard of "Death by Chocolate"? It's got nothing on this decadent cheesecake. In addition to adding liquid chocolate to the cake batter, we infuse it with chocolate liqueur. And there's no graham cracker crust here—we bake this one on a bed of crushed chocolate cookies. Chocolate lovers, rejoice!

Serves: 12 to 14 people

---

1 To prepare the crust, preheat the oven to 250°F. Coat the bottom and sides of a 9-inch springform pan with the room temperature butter.

2 In a medium bowl, mix the crushed cookies and melted butter until well blended. Press the crumb mixture into the bottom and halfway up the sides of the prepared pan. Wrap the pan in 2 layers of foil and bake for 7 minutes. Transfer to a wire rack to cool.

3 To prepare the ganache, in a bowl set over a saucepan of simmering water, stir the chocolate until melted and smooth.

4 In a small saucepan over medium heat, bring the cream and corn syrup just to a boil. Slowly mix the cream mixture into the melted chocolate. Set the ganache aside.

Active time:
60 minutes

Total time:
2 hours and 35 minutes,
plus at least 6 hours of
refrigeration time

CHOCOLATE COOKIE CRUST

Unsalted butter, at room temperature

10 ounces crushed Oreo cookies (1½ cups)

¾ stick (6 tablespoons) unsalted butter, melted

GANACHE

1 pound bittersweet chocolate, chopped

½ cup heavy cream

3 tablespoons light corn syrup

CHEESECAKE FILLING

Three 8-ounce packages Philadelphia® cream cheese, at room temperature

Pinch of regular salt

1 cup granulated sugar

4 large eggs

2 tablespoons cornstarch

2 tablespoons Godiva
  liqueur

1 tablespoon pure vanilla
  extract

1 cup sour cream

5 To prepare the filling, in the bowl of a stand mixer
   fitted with the paddle attachment, beat the cream
   cheese and salt on medium speed until smooth and
   fluffy. Scrape the bowl. Add the sugar and eggs
   and beat until blended. Add the cornstarch, Godiva
   liqueur, and vanilla and beat until blended. Add the
   ganache and beat until blended, about 1 minute.
   Increase the mixer speed to high. Add the sour cream
   and beat until smooth, about 30 seconds.

6 Pour the batter into the prepared crust and place
   the springform pan in a roasting pan. Pour enough
   boiling water into the roasting pan to come halfway
   up the sides of the springform pan. Bake until the
   filling is just set in the center, 70 to 75 minutes.

7 Remove from the oven and let cool in the roasting
   pan for 20 minutes. Transfer the springform pan to
   a wire rack to cool to room temperature. Refrigerate
   the cake overnight for it to set; do not remove the
   springform pan from the cheesecake until it has had
   at least 6 hours in the refrigerator to set.

JEAN

JEANETTE GASKINS HARRIS, GRANDMOM'S sister, never let grass grow under her feet. She always was—and still is, at age seventy-seven—a traveling woman.

A self-proclaimed "speedster," Jean often talked about how her uncles would let her drive the roads and highways surrounding Baltimore as a very young girl, age twelve or thirteen, when such things weren't so frowned upon or even considered dangerous. When Aunt Jean was a little older, in her midteens, her first foray onto the big city streets would leave an indelible mark; it was then when she had her first car accident.

As Aunt Jean tells the story, it was a warm, sunny day in the summer and a handsome young man, whose name she cannot remember any longer, was driving a "beautiful, red car," his first, and stopped in front of Jean "to show off." (Ever since this day, road trips and beaus, for Aunt Jean, have always gone hand in hand.) The young man asked her if she wanted to drive. "He didn't tell me where he wanted to go or even what to do," Aunt Jean said. "He just laid on back like he was sleeping."

But Jean had seen the way the cars in the city got around—fast and furious— and she was ready to do the same. She got behind a taxicab that whipped around a street corner, but when she tried to emulate the move, she lost control of the car, knocking over a lamppost. To make matters worse, when she drove back onto the street, she hit another car, scraping the young man's vehicle. "I was trying to hit the brakes and I kept hitting the gas, because I panicked," she said.

When Aunt Jean got a summons to appear in court, "everybody in the neighborhood knew about it and came to support me," she said. "They all got dressed up—my girlfriend even wore her fur coat—and filled up the courtroom. The judge said, 'Young lady, you go get your learner's permit, and don't drive in the city!'" He fined her thirty-five dollars.

When Aunt Jean finally got her license, there was no stopping her. Aunt Jean often traveled from Baltimore to Philadelphia, because it was the only way for her to stay close with her brothers and sister Elizabeth whom she had not grown up with—their ensuing tight bond was, in part, a result of her willingness to drive alone, if need be, for holidays and special occasions to be with them. Eventually, Aunt Jean moved to Philadelphia after she and her first husband separated in order to be closer to them, but she continues to drive every day. And when she's not driving, she's traveling by boat or plane or train.

I always love to hear Aunt Jean talk about her travels—her eyes grow wide with enthusiasm, which envelops her audience like a warm hug. Perhaps it's no coincidence that our red velvet cake (page 77), dedicated to a woman who was always on the go, is one of our most popular desserts—even now, Aunt Jean just won't stay put.

A WORD ON NUDIES

WE GOT THE IDEA FOR this line around 2008, the middle of the no-sugar-added craze. We were resistant, though, because sweeteners such as Splenda and aspartame went against what our bakery stood for, but then my mom got the idea to use fruit and juice instead, and the line became so popular that it grew from one cake to four. Because some folks were put off by the title "no sugar added," we decided to change the name to something a little sexier—nudies.

NUDIE CHOCOLATE BANANA CAKE WITH BLACKBERRY BUTTERCREAM

Serves: 8 people

1 Preheat the oven to 350°F. Coat two 6-inch round cake pans with nonstick cooking spray.

2 In a small saucepan over medium-high heat, bring the grape juice to a boil. Continue to boil until reduced to 1¼ cups. Cool to room temperature.

3 Meanwhile, in a medium bowl, whisk together the flour, cocoa powder, salt, cinnamon, nutmeg, allspice, and ginger.

4 In the bowl of a stand mixer fitted with the paddle attachment, beat the butter on medium speed until light and fluffy, about 3 minutes. Add the cooled reduced grape juice and beat until blended. Add the eggs, egg yolks, and vanilla and beat, scraping the bowl as necessary, until blended. Add the bananas and jam and beat until smooth.

Active time:
40 minutes

Total time:
1 hour and 25 minutes

Nonstick cooking spray with flour

1¾ cups 100% white grape juice

2½ cups all-purpose flour

¼ cup unsweetened cocoa powder

½ teaspoon regular salt

½ teaspoon ground cinnamon

½ teaspoon ground nutmeg

¼ teaspoon ground allspice

¼ teaspoon ground ginger

1½ sticks (12 tablespoons) unsalted butter, at room temperature

2 large eggs

2 large egg yolks

1 tablespoon pure vanilla extract

continued on the following page

5 In a small bowl, mix together the buttermilk and baking soda. Reduce the mixer speed to low and alternately add the flour mixture and buttermilk mixture to the butter mixture, mixing until blended. Increase the mixer speed to medium. Add ½ cup boiling water and beat until smooth.

6 Divide the batter equally between the prepared pans and bake until a wooden pick inserted into the center comes out clean, 40 to 45 minutes. Let the cakes cool in the pans for 10 minutes before turning them out onto a wire rack to cool completely.

7 To assemble and frost the cakes, place 1 cake layer, bottom-side up, on a cake plate. Use an offset spatula to spread 1 cup of the buttercream on top. Add the second cake layer, bottom-side up. Frost the top and sides of the cake with the remaining buttercream.

continued from page 111

2 small ripe bananas, peeled and mashed

⅓ cup no-sugar-added blackberry jam

⅓ cup buttermilk

2½ teaspoons baking soda

½ cup boiling water

1 recipe Nudie Blackberry Buttercream (recipe follows)

NUDIE BLACKBERRY BUTTERCREAM

Active time:
35 minutes

Total time:
55 minutes

Makes: 3½ cups

¾ cup 100% white grape juice

2 ounces Philadelphia® cream cheese, at room temperature

2¼ sticks (1 cup plus 2 tablespoons) unsalted butter, at room temperature

2 large egg yolks

¼ cup no-sugar-added blackberry jam, slightly warmed

1¼ teaspoons pure vanilla extract

1 In a small saucepan over medium-high heat, bring the grape juice to a boil. Continue to boil until reduced to ½ cup. Cool to room temperature.

2 Meanwhile, in the bowl of a stand mixer fitted with the paddle attachment, beat the cream cheese on medium speed until smooth, about 3 minutes.

3 Add the butter to the cream cheese and beat until fluffy, scraping the bowl as necessary, about 3 minutes. Increase the mixer speed to medium and beat until pale yellow and almost doubled in volume, scraping the bowl as necessary, about 6 minutes.

4 In another bowl of a stand mixer fitted with the whisk attachment, whisk the egg yolks on high speed until pale yellow, about 3 minutes. Reduce the mixer speed to low and slowly add the cooled reduced grape juice. Increase the mixer speed to high and beat until light and fluffy. Add the slightly warmed blackberry jam and vanilla extract and continue to whisk on high, about 5 minutes.

5 Replace the whisk attachment with the paddle attachment and reduce the mixer speed to medium. Add half of the whipped cream cheese–butter to the egg yolk mixture and beat until incorporated. Add the remaining whipped cream cheese–butter, increase the mixer speed to high, and beat until light and fluffy, scraping the bowl as necessary, about 5 minutes. Set aside until ready to use.

NUDIE HAZELNUT CAKE WITH ALMOND BUTTERCREAM

Active time:
35 minutes

Total time:
1 hour and 20 minutes

Serves: 8 people

1 Preheat the oven to 350°F. Coat two 6-inch round cake pans with nonstick cooking spray.

2 In a small saucepan over medium-high heat, bring the grape juice to a boil. Continue to boil until reduced to 1¼ cups. Cool to room temperature.

3 In a small cup, stir the hazelnut coffee and 2 tablespoons of the boiling water to blend.

4 In a medium bowl, whisk together the flour and salt.

5 In the bowl of a stand mixer fitted with the paddle attachment, beat the butter on medium-high speed until fluffy, scraping the bowl as necessary, about 3 minutes. Add the cooled reduced grape juice and beat until blended. Add the eggs and egg yolks, 1 at a time, beating until blended. Add the coffee mixture and vanilla to the batter and beat until just blended.

6 In a measuring cup, whisk together the buttermilk and baking soda. With the mixer on low speed,

Nonstick cooking spray with flour

1¾ cups 100% white grape juice

2½ teaspoons instant hazelnut-flavored coffee

2 tablespoons plus ¾ cup boiling water

2½ cups all-purpose flour

1 teaspoon regular salt

1½ sticks (12 tablespoons) unsalted butter, at room temperature

2 large eggs

2 large egg yolks

1½ tablespoons pure vanilla extract

¼ cup buttermilk

1½ tablespoons baking soda

1 recipe Nudie Almond Buttercream (recipe follows)

alternately add the flour mixture and buttermilk mixture to the batter, beginning and ending with the flour mixture and beating until smooth.

7 Slowly pour in the remaining ¾ cup of boiling water. Increase the mixer speed to medium-high and beat until incorporated.

8 Divide the batter equally between the prepared pans and bake until a wooden pick inserted into the center comes out clean, 40 to 45 minutes. Let the cakes cool in the pans for 10 minutes before turning them out onto a wire rack to cool completely.

9 To assemble and frost the cakes, place 1 cake layer, bottom-side up, on a cake plate. Use an offset spatula to spread 1 cup of the buttercream on top. Add the second cake layer, bottom-side up. Frost the top and sides of the cake with the remaining buttercream.

NUDIE ALMOND BUTTERCREAM

Makes: 6 cups

1 In a small saucepan over medium-high heat, bring the grape juice to a boil. Continue to boil until reduced to ½ cup. Cool to room temperature.

2 Meanwhile, in the bowl of a stand mixer fitted with the paddle attachment, beat the cream cheese on medium speed until light and fluffy, about 3 minutes.

3 Add the butter to the cream cheese and beat until fluffy, scraping the bowl as necessary, about 3 minutes. Increase the mixer speed to medium-high and beat until pale yellow and doubled in volume, scraping the bowl as necessary, about 4 minutes.

4 In another bowl of a stand mixer fitted with the whisk attachment, whisk the egg yolks on high speed until thick and pale yellow, about 3 minutes.

5 Reduce the mixer speed to low and slowly add the cooled reduced grape juice to the egg yolks. Increase the mixer speed to high and whisk until light and fluffy. Add the vanilla and almond extracts and continue to whisk on high, about 5 minutes.

6 Replace the whisk attachment with the paddle attachment and reduce the mixer speed to medium. Add half of the whipped cream cheese–butter to the egg yolk mixture and beat until incorporated. Add the remaining cream cheese–butter, increase the mixer speed to high, and beat until light and fluffy, scraping the bowl as necessary, about 5 minutes. Set aside until ready to use.

Active time:
35 minutes

Total time:
1 hour and 5 minutes

- ¾ cup 100% white grape juice

- 2 ounces Philadelphia® cream cheese, at room temperature

- 2½ sticks (1 cup plus 4 tablespoons) unsalted butter, at room temperature

- 2 large egg yolks

- 3 tablespoons pure vanilla extract

- ¾ teaspoon pure almond extract

NUDIE PUMPKIN CAKE WITH CREAM CHEESE BUTTERCREAM

Active time:
40 minutes

Total time:
1 hour and 25 minutes

Serves: 8 people

1 Preheat the oven to 350°F. Coat two 6-inch round cake pans with nonstick cooking spray.

2 In a medium saucepan over medium-high heat, bring the grape juice to a boil. Continue to boil until reduced to 1¼ cups. Cool to room temperature.

3 Meanwhile, in a medium bowl, whisk together the flour, salt, cinnamon, nutmeg, allspice, and ginger.

4 In the bowl of a stand mixer fitted with the paddle attachment, beat the butter until light and fluffy, about 3 minutes. Add the cooled reduced grape juice and beat, scraping the bowl as necessary, until blended. Add the eggs and egg yolks, 1 at a time, and vanilla, beating until blended. Add the pumpkin and applesauce and beat until smooth.

5 In a small bowl, mix the buttermilk and baking soda to blend.

Nonstick cooking spray with flour

1¾ cups 100% white grape juice

2½ cups all-purpose flour

½ teaspoon regular salt

1 teaspoon ground cinnamon

½ teaspoon ground nutmeg

¼ teaspoon ground allspice

¼ teaspoon ground ginger

1½ sticks (12 tablespoons) unsalted butter, at room temperature

2 large eggs

2 large egg yolks

1 tablespoon plus 2 teaspoons pure vanilla extract

12 ounce canned pumpkin purée

continued on the following page

6 Reduce the mixer speed to low and alternately add
   the flour mixture and the buttermilk mixture to
   the butter mixture, mixing just until incorporated.
   Increase the mixer speed to medium and beat in
   ¼ cup boiling water.

7 Divide the batter equally between the prepared pans.
   Bake until a wooden pick inserted into the center
   comes out clean, 40 to 45 minutes. Let the cakes cool
   in the pans for 10 minutes before turning them out
   onto a wire rack to cool completely.

8 To assemble and frost the cakes, place 1 cake layer,
   bottom-side up, on a cake plate. Use an offset spatula
   to spread 1 cup of the buttercream on top. Add the
   second cake layer, bottom-side up. Frost the top and
   sides of the cake with the remaining buttercream.

*continued from
page 119*

¼ cup unsweetened
   applesauce

¼ cup buttermilk

1 tablespoon plus 2
   teaspoons baking soda

¼ cup boiling water

1 recipe Nudie Cream
   Cheese Buttercream
   (recipe follows)

NUDIE CREAM CHEESE BUTTERCREAM

Makes: 3½ cups

1 In a small saucepan over medium-high heat, bring
   the grape juice to a boil. Continue to boil until
   reduced to ½ cup. Cool to room temperature.

2 Meanwhile, in the bowl of a stand mixer fitted with a whisk attachment, whisk the cream cheese on medium speed until light and fluffy, about 3 minutes.

3 Replace the whisk attachment with the paddle attachment and beat the butter into the cream cheese on medium speed, scraping the bowl as necessary, until light and fluffy. Increase the mixer speed to medium-high and beat until pale yellow and almost doubled in volume, scraping the bowl as necessary, about 4 minutes.

4 In another bowl of a stand mixer fitted with the whisk attachment, whisk the egg yolks on high speed until thick and a pale yellow, about 3 minutes.

5 Reduce the mixer speed to medium and add the cooled reduced grape juice to the egg yolks in a slow and steady stream until blended. Increase the mixer speed to high and whisk until very light and fluffy. On low speed, add the maple syrup and vanilla to the egg yolk mixture. Increase the mixer speed to high and whisk until smooth.

6 Add half of the whipped cream cheese–butter to the egg yolk mixture and whisk on medium speed until blended. Add the remaining whipped cream cheese–butter and cinnamon and whisk until fluffy, scraping the bowl as necessary, about 5 minutes. Set aside until ready to use.

Active time:
45 minutes

Total time:
60 minutes

- ¾ cup 100% white grape juice
- 3 ounces Philadelphia® cream cheese, at room temperature
- 2 sticks (1 cup) unsalted butter, at room temperature
- 2 large egg yolks
- 2 tablespoons sugar-free maple syrup
- 4 teaspoons pure vanilla extract
- Pinch of ground cinnamon

I COULD ALWAYS TELL the time of year by the pies and puddings made by my grandmom and mom. Apples pies meant fall. When I was in middle school, my family and I would drive out to Cheyney, Pennsylvania, every year to go apple picking for my birthday. Sure enough, we'd bring back a couple of extra bushels of apples to "share" with my grandmom, who would use them to make homemade applesauce as well as apple pie. In summer, the season of peaches, my mom would make large dishes of peach cobbler or peach pies for barbecues and graduation celebrations. And in the winter, our boots and mittens caked with ice, rice pudding would appear on our dining room table for dessert. This chapter is filled with these recipes as well as other vintage recipes from my family, including bread pudding and carrot pie, most of which marked the seasons of my childhood better than any weather forecast could.

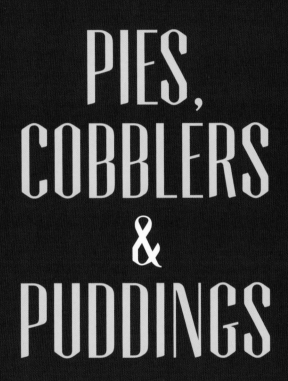

PIES, COBBLERS & PUDDINGS

APPLE BROWN BETTY

I have a confession to make: We didn't grow up eating Apple Brown Betty. It wasn't until the summer after we opened the bakery that my mom had time to research and develop a recipe for our own version of our namesake dessert. Made with three types of apples, a from-scratch rum sauce, and oat topping, our Apple Brown Betty may be somewhat prep-time intensive, but after tasting it served warm with ice cream, you'll wish you had started making it sooner.

Serves: 10 people

1   Preheat the oven to 350°F. Lightly butter a 9x13x2-inch baking dish.

2   To prepare the rum sauce, in a medium saucepan over medium-high heat, combine the water, sugar, butter, rum, cornstarch, and cinnamon, stirring frequently, until the sauce comes to a boil. Continue to cook, stirring occasionally, for 20 minutes. Set aside.

3   To prepare the crumb crust topping, in a large bowl, combine the oats, butter, flour, brown sugar, superfine sugar, and salt. With your hands, mix all the ingredients until large moist clumps form. Cover and refrigerate until ready to use.

Active time:
60 minutes

Total time:
2 hours and 15 minutes

RUM SAUCE

2 cups water

1 cup superfine sugar

½ stick (4 tablespoons) unsalted butter

2 tablespoons light rum

1 teaspoon cornstarch

1 teaspoon ground cinnamon

CRUMB CRUST TOPPING

½ cup old-fashioned oats

¾ stick (6 tablespoons) cold unsalted butter, cut into small pieces

6 tablespoons all-purpose flour

⅓ cup packed light brown sugar

4 tablespoons superfine sugar

Pinch of regular salt

continued on the following page

4 To prepare the potato bread crust, in another large bowl, toss the bread cubes with the melted butter and arrange two-thirds of the bread crumbs over the bottom of the prepared baking dish.

5 To prepare the apple mixture, fill a third large bowl with water and add the lemon juice. Halve, core, and slice all the apples, adding the slices to the lemon water as you go along to prevent them from browning.

6 In another large bowl, combine the raisins, brown sugar, superfine sugar, flour, lemon zest, cinnamon, nutmeg, and salt. Drain the lemon water from the apples, add the apples to the sugar and spice mixture, and toss to coat.

7 Place two-thirds of the apples on top of the bread cubes in the baking dish. Layer the remaining one-third of the bread cubes on top of the apples and follow with the remaining apples. Top with the butter pieces and 1½ cups of the rum sauce, and sprinkle with 1½ cups of the crumb topping. Cover and bake for 50 minutes. Remove from the oven and pour ½ cup more rum sauce and ½ cup more crumb topping over the casserole. Return to the oven uncovered and bake until the apples are soft and the topping is golden brown, about 20 minutes longer.

8 Serve warm with ice cream, if desired.

continued from page 125

POTATO BREAD CRUST

1 loaf potato bread, crusts removed, cut into 1-inch cubes

APPLE MIXTURE

1 tablespoon fresh lemon juice

7 Golden Delicious apples

5 Granny Smith apples

3 Red Delicious apples

½ cup raisins

½ cup packed light brown sugar

¼ cup superfine sugar

¼ cup all-purpose flour

1 tablespoon freshly grated lemon zest

½ teaspoon ground cinnamon

¼ teaspoon ground nutmeg

¼ teaspoon regular salt

½ stick (4 tablespoons) unsalted butter, cut into pieces

Vanilla ice cream

A WORD ON CRUST

EVERYONE WANTS A FLAKY, beautiful pie
crust and we have it. Our secrets are as
follows. First, we mix butter and shortening
together to make the dough. Second,
we chill the dough in the refrigerator for
at least 30 minutes before rolling it out.
Third, and as a result of all of the butter
added to the crust, we use a filler to prevent
the crust from shrinking while it pre-bakes.
This is a simple step. You simply place
a large, clean coffee filter on top of your
unbaked crust after you have lined the pan.
Then you pour a bag of beans (any will do)
on top of the liner to hold the crust in place.

ROSE

Rose Hinton Martin, Grandpop's sister, was the only one of five children, and the first among all our relatives, to go to college after high school. My grandmom and grandpop relied on Aunt Rose's schooling to guide the family and sought her counsel for most decisions, big and small, from how to handle a sensitive situation involving church politics to travel arrangements for family reunions.

After graduating from Cheyney Training School for Teachers, the oldest institution of higher learning for African-Americans, Rose took a teaching position in the Philadelphia public schools, where she worked for forty years, winning many awards. Years later, Rose would earn her doctorate in religion and become a minister.

A slim, "brown-skinned" woman who stood about 5 feet 5 inches tall, Rose was as fastidious about maintaining her figure and using medicinal herbs to "cleanse" her system as she was about education. Still, she loved to cook, bake, and entertain her family and friends. She especially liked to share her "friendship cake" starter featuring fruits, such as pineapples and peaches, which she would hand out in mason jars as gifts.

Rose's husband, Walter Martin Sr., also taught in the Philadelphia public schools for many years and was a wonderful, supportive husband. Walter was quiet and low-key and seemed to enjoy taking Rose on the Main Line anywhere she wanted or needed to go, such as flea markets and estate sales and farmers' markets on the weekend. Keeping up with Rose was no small feat—she was active in many organizations, including the Alpha Kappa Alpha Sorority, Inc., the oldest historically black sorority, which was very dear to her.

Outside of the classroom, Rose extolled the virtues of education to anyone who'd listen, particularly us children. She used to put my cousins and me in speaking contests where we would recite very long poems such as James Weldon Johnson's "The Creation." On weekends, we would spend the night at her house and practice for hours at a time to get our words and inflection just right. Aunt Rose said we had to learn to "express ourselves properly" and to perform—how to stand or sit, how to connect with the audience by "looking into their eyes." For years, she took us to every cultural arts program she could find, and when she couldn't find one we would just recite our newest poem at church service. She named our little troupe "Pinn Memorial's Speaking Trio."

By the time I went to high school, other extracurricular activities took time away from being able to rehearse for recitals, but the lessons Aunt Rose taught me about using public speaking as a tool have helped me greatly along my way—I raised the roof during my campaign for senior class president when I recited Maya Angelou's "Caged Bird."

Aunt Rose was such an important part of who I became, of who all of us became; we all walk a little taller buoyed by the knowledge she imparted. And when I see eager eyes ogling the rich chocolate raspberry cake (page 79) we've dedicated to her, sitting high on its glass pedestal, I could swear that I see it staring proudly right back.

DEEP-DISH APPLE PIE

When we say "deep dish," we really mean it. My grandmom would pile so many apples in her pie before she closed it up that I would worry we might not be able to roll out a top crust large enough to cover them all. But Grandmom could do anything with crust. Plus, the apples will cook down, and you don't want a flat pie—you want it to be high and remarkable and for everyone to ooh and aah when you carry it out from the kitchen. So just when you think you cannot fit any more apples, add a few more.

Serves: 6 to 8 people

---

1 Preheat the oven to 400°F.

2 On a lightly floured surface, roll out 1 of the pie crust doughs to a 12-inch-diameter round that is ⅛ inch thick and place it in a 9-inch deep-dish pie dish. Trim the dough along the edge, leaving a ½-inch overhang. Sprinkle 1 teaspoon of flour over the crust.

3 Roll out the remaining dough to a 12-inch-diameter round. Transfer the dough round to a parchment-lined baking sheet, and refrigerate both crusts.

4 In a large bowl, combine the apples with the lemon juice and toss to coat.

Active time:
45 minutes

Total time:
2 hours

- 2 recipes Pie Crust (see page 135)

- 1 teaspoon plus 3 tablespoons all-purpose flour, plus more for dusting

- 9 apples, such as Golden Delicious, Pink Lady, and Granny Smith, peeled, cored, and cut into ¾-inch-thick slices

- 1 tablespoon fresh lemon juice

- ½ cup granulated sugar

- ½ teaspoon ground cinnamon

- ¼ teaspoon ground nutmeg

- ¼ teaspoon regular salt

- ½ stick (4 tablespoons) cold unsalted butter, cut into small pieces

- ¼ cup whole milk

5 In a small bowl, whisk together the remaining
   3 tablespoons of flour, sugar, cinnamon, nutmeg,
   and salt.

6 Remove the pie pan from the refrigerator. Place half
   of the apples in the pie pan. Sprinkle half of the flour
   mixture over the apples. Place half of the butter on
   top. Repeat with the remaining apples, flour mixture,
   and butter.

7 Remove the top crust from the refrigerator and lay
   it over the top of the pie, then fold the edges under.
   Dip a fork in flour and use the tines to press down
   the crust and seal the edges. Use a paring knife to cut
   six 2-inch slits into the top crust. Use a pastry brush
   to brush enough milk over the top to coat the crust.
   Place the pie on a rimmed baking sheet.

8 Bake in the oven for 10 minutes. Reduce the oven
   temperature to 350°F and continue to bake the pie
   until the apples are tender and juice bubbles up
   around the crust, 45 to 55 minutes. Transfer the pie
   to a wire rack to cool to room temperature.

SWEET POTATO PIE

What would Thanksgiving be without sweet potato pie? It's a staple at bakeries, and even grocery stores, throughout the country. What makes ours unique? Weeks before Thanksgiving, my mom starts making small batch after batch of light and flaky crust, which she and her helpers meticulously add to each pan by hand. And our filling is made with real sweet potatoes and just the right amount of spice—not too compact, but not too airy either. The recipe has taken years to perfect, but to this day, every October, my mom pulls out the recipe to make sure we have it just right.

Serves: 2 pies; 6 to 8 servings each

1 Preheat the oven to 400°F. Line a rimmed baking sheet with foil.

2 Place the sweet potatoes on the baking sheet and rub the skins with oil. Roast the sweet potatoes until they are tender when pierced with a fork, 50 to 55 minutes. Let cool until easy enough to handle.

3 Using a knife, remove the skin of the sweet potatoes and place the flesh of the potatoes in the bowl of a stand mixer fitted with the paddle attachment. Beat the potato flesh on medium-high speed to remove pulp, about 1 minute. Push the flesh through a fine-mesh strainer over a medium bowl. Set aside. Reduce the oven temperature to 350°F.

Active time:
45 minutes

Total time:
2 hours and 25 minutes

- 3½ pounds sweet potatoes, scrubbed
- 2 tablespoons olive oil or vegetable oil
- 1½ sticks (¾ cup) unsalted butter, at room temperature
- 4 ounces Philadelphia® cream cheese, at room temperature
- ½ teaspoon regular salt
- ¾ cup granulated sugar
- ½ cup packed light brown sugar
- 3 large eggs
- ¾ teaspoon ground cinnamon
- ½ teaspoon ground nutmeg
- ¼ teaspoon ground allspice
- 1½ teaspoons pure vanilla extract
- ¼ cup heavy cream
- 2 recipes Pie Crust (see page 135), prebaked in two 9-inch deep-dish pie dishes

4 In another bowl of a stand mixer fitted with the paddle attachment, beat the butter, cream cheese, and salt on medium speed until fluffy, about 3 minutes. Add the granulated sugar and brown sugar and beat until well blended. Add the eggs, 1 at a time, beating until blended.

5 Add the mashed sweet potatoes, cinnamon, nutmeg, allspice, vanilla, and cream and beat until smooth.

6 Pour the mixture into the prebaked pie crusts and bake for 10 minutes. Reduce the oven temperature to 325°F and bake until the centers are set, about 55 minutes. Transfer the pies to a wire rack to cool completely.

PIE CRUST

- 2 cups all-purpose flour, plus more for dusting
- 3 tablespoons granulated sugar
- ¼ teaspoon regular salt
- 1 ½ sticks (12 tablespoons) cold unsalted butter, cut into pieces
- 4 tablespoons vegetable shortening
- 1 ounce Philadelphia® cream cheese
- 1 large egg yolk
- 2 tablespoons ice water, plus more if needed

1 Preheat the oven to 425°F. In a large bowl, whisk together the flour, sugar, and salt. Use your fingers to mix the butter, shortening, and cream cheese into the flour mixture until it looks like coarse crumbs.

2 Use your hands to mix the egg yolk and 2 table-spoons ice water into the crumb mixture. Check the consistency of the dough by squeezing a small amount between your thumb and forefingers. The dough should hold together. If the mixture is dry, add more water, 1 teaspoon at a time, to reach the desired consistency.

3 Shape the dough into a disk, wrap it in plastic, and refrigerate for at least 1 hour or up to 5 days.

4 On a lightly floured surface, roll out the dough to ⅛-inch thickness and place it in a 9-inch deep-dish pie dish. Trim the dough along the edge, leaving a ½- to ¾-inch overhang. Pinch to form a decorative edge. Use the tines of a fork to prick the crust on the bottom. Refrigerate until set, about 30 minutes.

5 To prebake, line the crust with parchment paper and fill with pie weights or baking beans. Bake in a preheated 425°F oven for 10 minutes. Transfer to a wire rack to cool completely.

LEMON MERINGUE PIE

My grandmom loves lemon meringue pie. During her "supper club" days, a big piece of refreshing lemon meringue pie would always come out after a nice steak dinner. These days, it's hard to find lemon meringue pie at a bakery—even ours. We don't carry it, because it's difficult to get the meringue to hold up while waiting for a customer to purchase it, but if you're like Grandmom and have a hankering for lemon meringue from time to time—perhaps for your own supper club— now you can make it yourself.

Serves: 6 to 8 people

1 Preheat the oven to 350°F.

2 In a medium bowl, lightly whisk the egg yolks.

3 In a medium double boiler over medium heat, stir together the sugar, cornstarch, flour, and salt. Gradually add ¼ cup plus 2 tablespoons of the lemon juice and stir to blend. Add 1 cup boiling water and the milk and cook, stirring constantly, until the mixture forms a mound when dropped from a spoon, about 12 minutes. Remove from the heat.

4 Add ¼ cup of the milk mixture to the egg yolks while whisking constantly. Continuing to whisk, pour the egg mixture into the remaining milk mixture in the and cook until thickened, stirring constantly, 2 to 3 minutes. Remove from the heat.

Active time:
35 minutes

Total time:
50 minutes

3 large egg yolks

¾ cup granulated sugar

¼ cup plus 2 tablespoons cornstarch

1 tablespoon all-purpose flour

¼ teaspoon regular salt

¼ cup plus 3 tablespoons fresh lemon juice

1 cup boiling water

1 cup evaporated milk

3 tablespoons unsalted butter

½ teaspoon freshly grated lemon zest

1 recipe Pie Crust (see page 135), prebaked in a 9-inch deep-dish pie dish

1 recipe Meringue Pie Topping (recipe follows)

5 Add the butter, lemon zest, and remaining 1 table-spoon of lemon juice and stir until blended. Set aside to cool. Pour the lemon filling into the prebaked pie crust.

6 Use an offset spatula to spread the meringue over the lemon filling, making sure it touches the crust all around.

7 Bake until the meringue begins to brown, 10 to 15 minutes. Transfer the pie to a wire rack to cool completely. Refrigerate for 2 hours.

Meringue Pie Topping

Makes: 2 cups

Active time:
12 minutes

Total time:
17 minutes

½ cup granulated sugar

¼ cup packed light brown sugar

3 large egg whites

¼ teaspoon cream of tartar

Pinch of regular salt

1 In a medium bowl, whisk together the granulated sugar and brown sugar to blend. Set aside.

2 In the bowl of a stand mixer fitted with the whisk attachment, whisk the egg whites, cream of tartar, and salt on medium speed until foamy, about 2 minutes.

3 Continue to whisk on medium speed, gradually adding the sugar mixture, 2 tablespoons at a time, until blended.

4 Increase the mixer speed to high and whisk the egg white mixture until stiff, glossy peaks form, about 3 minutes. Use immediately.

COCONUT CREAM PIE

Some things just do not need to be messed around with because they are pretty great as is. That's how we feel about coconut cream pie. Have you ever tasted one you didn't like? I haven't. So ours is pretty classic. We make it just a bit creamier than most and perhaps add just a bit more coconut for good measure. Otherwise, we think why mess with a good thing?

Serves: 6 to 8 people

1 Preheat the oven to 375°F.

2 Spread ½ cup of the coconut on a small baking sheet. Bake the coconut, stirring occasionally, until it just begins to brown, about 6 minutes. Cool to room temperature.

3 In a medium double boiler, whisk together the remaining ⅓ cup sugar, cornstarch, flour, and salt. Gradually add the whole milk and evaporated milk to the sugar mixture, whisking until blended. Cook over medium heat stirring frequently, until the mixture begins to boil, thickens, and forms a mound when dropped from a spoon, about 12 minutes. Remove from the heat.

4 In a medium bowl, whisk the egg yolks and remaining ⅓ cup of sugar until smooth. Add ¼ cup of the milk mixture to the egg yolks and whisk until

Active time:
35 minutes

Total time:
50 minutes

- 1½ cups sweetened flaked coconut
- ⅔ cup granulated sugar
- ¼ cup plus 2 tablespoons cornstarch
- 1 tablespoon all-purpose flour
- ¼ teaspoon regular salt
- 1 cup whole milk
- 1 cup evaporated milk
- 3 large egg yolks
- 2 tablespoons unsalted butter
- 1½ teaspoons pure vanilla extract
- 1 recipe Pie Crust (see page 135), prebaked in a 9-inch deep-dish pie dish
- Sweetened Whipped Cream (optional; recipe follows)

blended. Pour the egg mixture into the remaining milk mixture in the double boiler and cook until very thick, stirring constantly, 1 to 2 minutes. Remove from the heat.

5 Stir in the butter, vanilla, and remaining 1 cup of coconut. Mix until well blended.

6 Pour the custard into the prebaked pie crust and top with the remaining coconut. Transfer the pie to a wire rack to cool to room temperature. Refrigerate for at least 1 hour. Top the pie with Sweetened Whipped Cream, if desired.

Sweetened Whipped Cream

Makes: 2½ cups

1 Chill the bowl and paddle of a stand mixer in the freezer for 20 minutes. Remove the bowl and paddle and immediately beat the cream on high speed until frothy.

2 Add the sugar and vanilla and beat until soft peaks form, about 3 minutes. Use immediately or refrigerate in an airtight container for up to 4 hours.

Active time:
10 minutes

Total time:
20 minutes

1 cup heavy cream

¼ cup confectioners' sugar or 2 tablespoons granulated sugar

½ teaspoon pure vanilla extract

PUMPKIN PIE

We grew up on sweet potato pie, not pumpkin pie. When we opened the bakery, however, a lot of our new neighbors kept asking for pumpkin pie instead. For years, my mom resisted going into that unfamiliar territory, and the neighborhood learned to love her sweet potato pies. (We still cannot make enough for Thanksgiving.) But when it came to thinking of additional recipes for this book, my mom took to the kitchen and decided to give pumpkin a go. Who knew? It is great too. And guess what's on our Thanksgiving menu now, right next to its sweet potato cousin?

Serves: 8 to 10 people

1 Preheat the oven to 450°F.

2 In the bowl of a stand mixer fitted with the paddle attachment, blend together the butter, brown sugar, granulated sugar, and salt until smooth. Add the eggs and pumpkin purée and stir until blended. Add the cinnamon, ginger, nutmeg, cloves, rum, milk, and ½ cup water and blend until smooth.

3 Pour the pumpkin filling into the prebaked pie crust and bake for 15 minutes. Reduce the oven temperature to 350°F and bake for 15 minutes. Reduce the oven temperature to 300°F and continue to bake until the center of the pie is set, about 30 minutes. Transfer the pie to a wire rack to cool completely.

Active time:
40 minutes

Total time:
1 hour and 40 minutes

- 1 stick (8 tablespoons) unsalted butter, melted
- ¾ cup packed light brown sugar
- ¼ cup granulated sugar
- ½ teaspoon regular salt
- 3 large eggs, lightly beaten
- 2 cups freshly cooked or canned pumpkin purée
- 2 teaspoons ground cinnamon
- 2 teaspoons ground ginger
- 1 teaspoon ground nutmeg
- ¼ teaspoon ground cloves
- 1 tablespoon rum or 1 tablespoon dark molasses
- 1 cup evaporated milk
- ½ cup water
- 1 recipe Pie Crust (see page 135), prebaked in a 9-inch deep-dish pie dish

CARROT PIE

In preparation for this book, we began thinking about some vintage recipes that we don't make in the bakery but might be good additions to a home baker's repertoire. One of the first recipes we thought of, on Aunt Jean's suggestion, was carrot pie. Not only is it delightful, but it doesn't require many unusual ingredients, so this is one you can whip up last minute.

Serves: 8 to 10 people

1 Preheat the oven to 425°F.

2 Bring a medium pot of water to a boil, add the carrots, and boil covered until soft, about 30 minutes. Drain. In a medium bowl, use a potato masher to mash the cooked carrots. Place a fine-mesh strainer over another medium bowl. Use a wooden spoon to push the mashed carrots through the strainer and into the bowl. You will need about 1¼ cups of mashed carrots. Set aside.

3 In the bowl of a stand mixer fitted with the paddle attachment, beat the butter and salt on medium speed until fluffy, about 3 minutes. Reduce the mixer speed to medium-low speed. Add the brown sugar, granulated sugar, and flour and beat until blended.

Active time:
50 minutes

Total time:
2 hours

7 to 9 carrots, peeled

1 stick (8 tablespoons) unsalted butter, at room temperature

½ teaspoon regular salt

¾ cup packed light brown sugar

¼ cup granulated sugar

3 tablespoons all-purpose flour

2 large eggs

1 large egg yolk

1½ teaspoons pure vanilla extract

¼ cup finely grated carrots

1 tablespoon dark molasses

2 teaspoons fresh lemon juice

1½ teaspoons ground cinnamon

1 teaspoon ground ginger

continued on the following page

4 Add the eggs, egg yolk, and vanilla and beat until well blended, scraping the bowl as necessary. Add the mashed carrots and grated carrots and beat until blended.

5 Add the molasses, lemon juice, cinnamon, ginger, nutmeg, and cloves and beat until well blended. Add the milk and cream and beat until smooth, scraping the bowl as necessary.

6 Pour the batter into the prebaked pie crust and bake for 10 minutes. Reduce the oven temperature to 350°F and continue to bake until the center of the pie is set, about 40 minutes. Transfer the pie to a wire rack to cool completely.

continued from page 143

½ teaspoon ground nutmeg

¼ teaspoon ground cloves

½ cup evaporated milk

½ cup heavy cream

1 recipe Pie Crust (see page 135), prebaked in a 9-inch deep-dish pie dish

BREAD PUDDING

This is one of the desserts we started experimenting with for the cookbook, and, in the interim, it has transcended to the bakery menu. At first, I thought it was too similar in taste and texture to Apple Brown Betty (which already has such a huge following) to be worth the effort, but the beauty of this recipe is that it's a lot easier to make—fewer steps and fewer ingredients—making it the perfect choice for when your fall sweet tooth is calling and time is of the essence.

Serves: 10 people

1 Preheat the oven to 350°F. Lightly coat an 8x8x2-inch baking dish with 1 tablespoon of the butter.

2 Place the bread cubes on a rimmed baking sheet and toast them in the oven until golden brown, about 8 minutes.

3 In the bowl of a stand mixer fitted with the paddle attachment, beat the remaining 1 stick of butter on medium-high speed until creamy. Add the granulated sugar and brown sugar and beat on low speed until light and fluffy, about 3 minutes. Add the eggs, 1 at a time, beating until blended. On low speed, add the dried fruit, brandy, vanilla, cinnamon, and nutmeg and mix until blended.

Active time:
35 minutes

Total time:
1 hour and 10 minutes

1 tablespoon plus 1 stick (8 tablespoons) unsalted butter, at room temperature

12 slices cinnamon-raisin bread, cut into 1-inch cubes

¾ cup granulated sugar

¼ cup packed light brown sugar

3 large eggs

¼ cup chopped dried fruit, such as apricots, cranberries, or golden raisins

2 tablespoons brandy

1½ teaspoons pure vanilla extract

1 teaspoon ground cinnamon

¼ teaspoon ground nutmeg

One 12-ounce can evaporated milk

½ cup heavy cream

4 In a medium bowl, combine the milk and cream. Fold the bread cubes into the milk mixture and continue to mix until most of the liquid has been absorbed by the bread. Pour the butter mixture into the bread mixture and mix well.

5 Transfer the pudding mixture to the prepared baking dish and bake until the bread pudding is golden brown and a wooden pick inserted into the center comes out clean, about 35 minutes. Transfer the bread pudding to a wire rack to cool for 20 minutes before serving.

PEACH COBBLER

Customers call all the time about our peach cobbler, wondering if we are "carrying it yet," only to be told (depending on the season) my mom's standard reply: "The peaches haven't gotten sweet enough yet." Most folks don't realize that we shop for peaches at produce and farmers' markets (which we also recommend you do, for best results) only when they are in season and buy them only when they are ripe and sweet. No frozen or canned peaches here. So they have to wait. As I did growing up. Because there's nothing better than when my mom finally deems a season's peaches "suitable" and out comes container after container of golden, sweet deliciousness, topped with light, fluffy dumplings.

Serves: 6 people

1 Preheat the oven to 350°F. Coat a 9x13x2-inch baking dish with 1 tablespoon of the butter.

2 Bring a large pot of water to a boil and prepare an ice water bath. Cut a small X into the bottom of each peach. Boil the peaches for 1 minute, then transfer them to the ice water bath. Once cool, peel and pit the peaches. Cut each peach into 8 slices and place them in a medium bowl.

3 Toss the peaches with ¼ cup of the granulated sugar, the brown sugar, and lemon juice and let stand until juices form, tossing several times, about 30 minutes.

Active time:
40 minutes

Total time:
2 hours

1 tablespoon plus ½ stick (4 tablespoons) unsalted butter

8 large peaches

¼ cup plus 2 tablespoons granulated sugar

¼ cup packed light brown sugar

1 teaspoon fresh lemon juice

2 tablespoons peach or apricot brandy

2 teaspoons cornstarch

¾ teaspoon ground cinnamon

½ teaspoon ground ginger

½ teaspoon ground nutmeg

¼ teaspoon regular salt

3 slices potato bread, cubed

1 recipe Cobbler Topping (recipe follows)

4 In a small bowl, whisk together the brandy, cornstarch, ½ teaspoon of the cinnamon, the ginger, nutmeg, and salt. Add this mixture to the peaches and toss to coat.

5 Place the bread cubes on a rimmed baking sheet and bake until golden brown, tossing once, about 8 minutes. Place the bread cubes on the bottom of the prepared baking pan and top with the peach mixture. Dot the peaches with the remaining ½ stick of butter.

6 Loosely cover the pan with foil. Place the pan on a rimmed baking sheet and bake until cooked through and the juices are bubbling, about 45 minutes.

7 Remove the baking pan from the oven and top the peaches with spoonfuls of the Cobbler Topping. Sprinkle with the remaining 2 tablespoons of granulated sugar and ¼ teaspoon of cinnamon.

8 Bake, uncovered, until the juices start to bubble up over the crust, about 20 minutes. Cool slightly and serve.

Cobbler Topping

Makes: 2 cups

Active time:
10 minutes

Total time:
15 minutes

1 In a medium bowl, whisk together the flour, sugar, baking powder, baking soda, salt, cinnamon, ginger, and nutmeg. Use 2 forks or your fingers to mix the butter into the flour

2 Add the buttermilk and vanilla and mix until blended. The mixture will resemble a thick batter.

1½ cups all-purpose flour

¾ cup granulated sugar

1 tablespoon baking powder

½ teaspoon baking soda

½ teaspoon regular salt

½ teaspoon ground cinnamon

⅛ teaspoon ground ginger

⅛ teaspoon ground nutmeg

1 stick (8 tablespoons) cold unsalted butter, cut into small pieces

¾ cup buttermilk

¾ teaspoon pure vanilla extract

ALICE GASKINS

GRANDMOM'S SISTER-IN-LAW, ALICE CLEO Crawford, was happiest when she was directing and singing in the church choir. Everyone in the family called her "Little Alice"—to distinguish her from Grandmom's cousin, Alice Corbin, who was affectionately dubbed "Big Alice"—but there was nothing small about her voice, which was boisterous and lively and almost mismatched for such a petite woman.

Aunt Alice served as director of music for Bethany Baptist Church on 58th Street and Warrington Avenue, where, in addition to singing, she played the organ and piano for thirty-one years. She was known for her booming solos, which resounded in that big city church, filled to capacity every Sunday, raising everyone's spirits as well as their hands, which would clap along in rhythm.

Having received some formal vocal training at community college as well as at Temple and Hampton Universities, Aunt Alice worked at Baker's Funeral Home for twenty-one years. She could often be seen standing at the front door, greeting folks who had come to grieve, and as soon as memorial services began, she would be front and center singing and playing the organ—her voice tender and comforting to those in mourning.

Alice's favorite songs to sing were religious hymns, and she would take every opportunity to sing them, whether at work or at church or at home. Often, someone in the family would call out "C'mon, Alice, sing us a song," and Alice would get right up and belt out a tune with such verve and confidence that everyone's hearts would swell.

Aunt Alice met Uncle Buster at Pinn Memorial Baptist Church when they were just teenagers, not long after he returned home to Philadelphia from serving in the military. (Uncle Buster had moved his age up, so that he could serve in World War II along with his older brother Chris.) After about a year of courtship, they wed in a big church ceremony—replete with a big dress and a very big wedding party—and remained happily married for sixty-one years.

Although Aunt Alice and Uncle Buster had no children themselves, they helped raise a host of children in their families and their godchildren. They helped pay for their textbooks, college tuitions, and sometimes bought them cars so that they could travel back and forth to school or work. My grandpop never was one for much highway driving, so, at the start and end of every school year, Uncle Buster and Aunt Alice would drive my mother, Linda, back and forth to Northampton, Massachusetts, where she attended Smith College.

Aunt Alice and Uncle Buster always kept a pair of shiny Cadillacs parked at the curb so that they could run errands or go visiting separately—Alice loved to drive, particularly to visit her grandmother who lived in Alabama. But mostly they liked to travel together. They often drove to Virginia to visit family, and on occasion headed farther to Atlanta, or cross-country to California and Nevada to "see the world," as Uncle Buster would say. The two also liked to paint the local town red, eating at nice restaurants, which they did often.

As a tribute to Aunt Alice, and to her life with Uncle Buster, we've dedicated our marble pound cake (page 73): The play of light and dark batter may vary, depending upon the slice, but they're always there together, like those two Cadillacs parked side by side.

SWEET POTATO PUDDING

My grandmom made this pudding every week with no exception. My grandpop and mom enjoyed it so much that she had to keep it in the house at all times. Simple and versatile, it can be a side dish or a dessert, and served hot, cold, or at room temperature.

Serves: 12 people

1 Arrange the oven rack in the lower third of the oven. Preheat the oven to 400°F. Line a rimmed baking sheet with foil.

2 Rub the potatoes with vegetable oil and place them on the prepared baking sheet. Bake the potatoes on the lower rack of the oven until fork tender, 50 to 55 minutes. Let cool until easy enough to handle. Peel the potatoes.

3 In the bowl of a stand mixer fitted with the paddle attachment, beat the cream cheese on medium speed until fluffy. Add the potatoes and beat until smooth. Use a spoon to push the mixture through a fine-mesh strainer and into a medium bowl.

4 Transfer the potatoes back to the bowl of the stand mixer fitted with the paddle attachment. Add the butter and salt and beat until smooth, about 3 minutes. Add the granulated sugar and brown sugar

Active time:
1 hour and 30 minutes

Total time:
2 hours and 20 minutes

5 pounds sweet potatoes, scrubbed

3 tablespoons vegetable oil

One 8-ounce package Philadelphia® cream cheese, at room temperature

1 stick (8 tablespoons) unsalted butter, at room temperature

¼ teaspoon regular salt

1¼ cups granulated sugar

½ cup packed light brown sugar

5 large eggs

¼ cup evaporated milk

1 tablespoon fresh orange juice

1½ teaspoons pure vanilla extract

½ teaspoon ground nutmeg

Vegetable shortening

1 teaspoon ground cinnamon

A WORD ON SWEET POTATOES

BEFORE WE OPENED THE BAKERY, we had no idea how few people baked with sweet potatoes. We use sweet potatoes a lot at the bakery and in this book, so just in case you are new to using sweet potatoes in baking, here are a couple of tips to help you along. The main point of all of this is to get as much of the pulp out as possible. We achieve our smooth batters by straining them over and over again. The extra time is worth it. Trust us. You will want to use the paddle attachment of your stand mixer to whip the skinned, roasted sweet potatoes. Do this once for 30 seconds and then discard all of the pulp that will have gathered on your paddle. Repeat this step and then move on to making your batter as directed in the recipe. Once your batter is made, you should hand strain the batter to remove any remaining pulp and lumps. All of this straining is guaranteed to get you one smooth sweet potato filling.

and beat until blended. Add the eggs, 1 at a time, beating until incorporated. Add the milk, orange juice, vanilla, and nutmeg and beat until the pudding batter is smooth.

5 Position the rack in the center of the oven. Coat the bottom and sides of a 9x13x2-inch baking pan with vegetable shortening and set the pan on a baking sheet.

6 Pour the pudding batter into the prepared baking pan and sprinkle the top with cinnamon. Bake in the middle of the oven until the pudding is set in the center, 45 to 50 minutes. Transfer the pudding to a wire rack to cool for 15 minutes before serving. Serve at room temperature or cold.

RICE PUDDING

I begged my grandmom to make her rice pudding whenever I got the chance. With its creamy top and perfectly cooked rice, it had just the right amount of cinnamon and nutmeg. Now that I'm a baker myself, I understand why she didn't make it more often—it takes a bit of time and doesn't keep well. Although our rice pudding is perfect for special days and every day, be sure to make it when there are guests coming who can help polish it off in a day or two.

Active time:
30 minutes

Total time:
2 hours and 30 minutes

1 tablespoon plus ¾ stick (6 tablespoons) unsalted butter

4½ cups whole milk

¾ teaspoon regular salt

¾ cup long-grain white rice

5 large egg yolks

2 teaspoons pure vanilla extract

1 cup granulated sugar

1½ teaspoons cornstarch

1 teaspoon freshly grated lemon zest

½ teaspoon ground nutmeg

¼ teaspoon ground cinnamon

1 cup heavy cream

Serves: 10 people

1 Preheat the oven to 350°F. Coat a 9x13x2-inch casserole dish with 1 tablespoon of the butter. Prepare a cool water bath.

2 Combine the milk and ½ teaspoon of the salt in the top of a double boiler (with simmering water in the bottom to prevent scorching) over medium heat. Add the rice and cook, uncovered, for 20 minutes. Cover the double boiler and cook for an additional 25 minutes or until the rice is still tender yet firm. Set the top of the double boiler into the water bath and stir the rice to cool the mixture and stop the cooking process.

3 While the rice is cooking, in a medium bowl, whip the egg yolks briefly, then stir in the vanilla.

4 In another medium bowl, mix the sugar, cornstarch, lemon zest, nutmeg, cinnamon, and the remaining ¼ teaspoon of salt. Add this spice mixture to the egg yolk mixture and stir until well blended.

5 Pour the cooked rice mixture into a large bowl. Add the egg mixture, heavy cream, and remaining ¾ stick of butter and stir until well blended.

6 Pour the rice pudding mixture into the prepared casserole dish. Set the casserole dish in a larger roasting pan and add enough water to the roasting pan to come halfway up the sides of the casserole dish. Bake for 1 hour and 10 minutes.

7 Remove the roasting pan from the oven (with the casserole dish still in the roasting pan) and let stand for 10 minutes. Remove the casserole dish from the roasting pan and set it on a cooling rack. Cool the pudding for 1 hour at room temperature, then refrigerate the pudding until it is completely chilled.

ALICE CORBIN

ALICE CORBIN, OR "BIG ALICE," as she was called, loved to dance.

Alice was married to Grandmom's cousin, Warren Corbin, Dot's twin brother, and together she and Warren were the Ginger Rogers and Fred Astaire of their tight-knit community. Tall and slim, Alice had long hair that fell down the middle of her back, and, paired with Warren, who had short, wavy hair and light green eyes, they made a striking couple when they took the dance floor at social and family gatherings. A wide circle would form around them, and people would stop what they were doing just to admire their moves. The stories I heard growing up painted a picture of Aunt Alice, in her very high-heeled shoes, gliding across the floor as if on a cloud, and as the music played, she and Uncle Warren would cover every square inch of that floor doing the jitterbug, the bossa nova, or the bop— whatever dance happened to be in style at the time.

Aunt Alice and Uncle Warren loved to be around people and did lots of entertaining in the 1960s. On Saturday nights, they had a dance instructor named Jerome come to their home and give lessons to about twelve couples in their basement. And every Friday evening, Alice would host her famous pinochle parties. My grandmom and grandpop and lots of other couples would get dressed up, go around to their house after dinner, and listen to music, dance in the living room, and play cards. Aunt Alice was the queen of pinochle—she rarely lost a game. These parties lasted until the wee hours of the morning, nothing but fun and laughter as Aunt Alice and her partner "rubbed head after head" while the young people, like my mom and Cousin Crystal, Alice and Warren's daughter, hung out all night on the front porch. It was actually on one of those nights that my parents met—my dad passed by with a friend on his way home and noticed my mom sitting on the porch with her cousins.

Big Alice worked for the Veteran's Administration downtown, and every weekday evening you could hear the clickety-clack of her high heels (in those days, virtually all the women seemed to wear high heels as part of their daily attire) when she stepped off the forty-six bus coming home from work. Cousin Crystal used to run around the corner to meet her, because she knew her mother would always have a little treat in her pocketbook. Back then, all the women seemed to have a certain sass and class about them, but none of them could move like Big Alice.

Cousin Crystal has often said that the first time she saw her own husband at a party in the basement of a mutual friend, he walked up to her and asked her to bop—that's when she knew he was the one. Big Alice made music a part of the lives of all who surrounded her, so we named one of our pound cakes "Alice's Two-Step" as a tribute to a woman who lived life to the fullest both on and off the dance floor.

Try one as part of a homemade ice cream sandwich.

CHRISTMAS COOKIES WERE A big tradition in my house. My mom didn't just make them for my dad, my sister, and me; she made enough for the entire family on both sides—aunts, uncles, cousins, friends, and neighbors. If Santa was good to them— and he was every year—they expected to get a tin of Linda's cookies on top of whatever other presents might be coming their way. In preparation for baking, my mom spent much of December tearing out cookie recipes and stocking up on bags of chocolate chips and coconut flakes from the local supermarkets. And on the first day of Christmas vacation—my mom has been a teacher in the Philadelphia public schools for over thirty years—there she was, planted in the kitchen, pulling out tray after tray of cookies, and organizing them by type on the dining room table until it was time to start packing the tins. We had to eat out most of that week leading up to Christmas, which was a rarity, but none of us complained—we were too busy sneaking a cookie here and there. In this chapter, you'll find some of our favorite cookie recipes my mom amassed over the years. They are all pretty simple and actually ideal for any season or reason: Try the double chocolate in the summertime as part of a homemade ice cream sandwich and the oatmeal raisin in the fall washed down with some fresh cider.

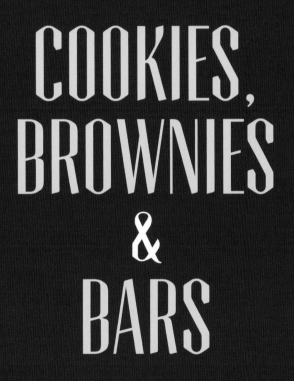

COOKIES, BROWNIES & BARS

CHOCOLATE CHIP COOKIES WITH WALNUTS

Active time:
30 minutes

Total time:
45 minutes

Chocolate chip cookies may be universally loved, but their taste varies so widely from one baker to the next. Our cookies are just right—not too soft, not too hard, with the perfect amount of chocolate. But if you prefer a softer version, we suggest you bake them a couple of minutes less (for a crisper version, a couple of minutes more). Consider this a launching pad for developing your own family's perfect recipe.

Makes: 16 cookies

1 Arrange the oven racks in the upper and lower thirds of the oven. Preheat the oven to 350°F. Line 3 baking sheets with parchment paper.

2 In a medium bowl, whisk together the flour, baking soda, and salt.

3 In the bowl of a stand mixer fitted with the paddle attachment, beat the butter, shortening, granulated sugar, brown sugar, sour cream, and vanilla on medium speed until smooth, about 3 minutes.

4 Add the egg and beat until blended. Add the flour mixture and beat until smooth. Stir in the chocolate chips and nuts, if desired.

1½ cups all-purpose flour

½ teaspoon baking soda

½ teaspoon regular salt

½ stick (4 tablespoons) unsalted butter, at room temperature

¼ cup vegetable shortening

¾ cup granulated sugar

¾ cup packed light brown sugar

1½ teaspoons sour cream

1 teaspoon pure vanilla extract

1 large egg

¾ cup semisweet chocolate chips

¼ cup chopped walnuts, toasted, optional (see page 84)

5 Using ¼ cup of dough for each cookie, place the cookies 3 inches apart on the prepared baking sheets. Bake the cookies until they are golden brown, rotating the pans halfway through, 10 to 12 minutes.

6 Let the cookies cool on the baking sheets for 10 minutes before transferring them to wire racks to cool completely.

OATMEAL RAISIN COOKIES

Oatmeal raisin cookies are essential to any bakery, but we like adding coconut to this recipe to switch it up a bit and because it's a nice addition to the texture and keeps the cookies surprisingly moist. Of course, if you prefer your oatmeal cookies the traditional way, just omit the coconut. It's still an oldie, but a goodie.

Makes: 18 cookies

1 Preheat the oven to 350°F. Line 3 baking sheets with parchment paper.

2 In a medium bowl, whisk together the flour, baking soda, cinnamon, and salt.

Active time:
30 minutes

Total time:
45 minutes

1¾ cups all-purpose flour

1 teaspoon baking soda

1 teaspoon ground cinnamon

½ teaspoon regular salt

2 sticks (1 cup) unsalted butter, at room temperature

1 cup packed light brown sugar

½ cup granulated sugar

¼ cup whole milk

2 large eggs

2 teaspoons pure vanilla extract

3 cups old-fashioned oats

1 cup raisins

¾ cup sweetened flaked coconut

3 In the bowl of a stand mixer fitted with the paddle attachment, beat the butter, brown sugar, granulated sugar, milk, eggs, and vanilla on medium speed until light and fluffy, about 3 minutes.

4 Stir the flour mixture into the butter mixture by hand. Stir in the oats, raisins, and coconut.

5 Using a scant ¼ cup of dough for each cookie, drop the dough 3 inches apart onto the prepared baking sheets. Bake until the cookies are golden brown around the edges, about 10 minutes.

6 Let the cookies cool on the baking sheets for 10 minutes before transferring them to wire racks to cool completely.

PEANUT BUTTER COOKIES

These peanut butter cookies are a fall favorite at the bakery. They are buttery with a bit of crunch around the outside and a bit soft in the center, making them just as perfect for tailgate parties as for middle school bake sales.

Makes: 20 cookies

Active time:
35 minutes

Total time:
1 hour and 17 minutes

2½ cups all-purpose flour

1½ teaspoons baking soda

1 teaspoon baking powder

½ teaspoon regular salt

2 sticks (1 cup) unsalted butter, at room temperature

1 cup smooth peanut butter

1 cup granulated sugar

1 cup packed light brown sugar

2 large eggs

1 teaspoon pure vanilla extract

1 Arrange the oven racks in the upper and lower thirds of the oven. Preheat the oven to 350°F. Line 3 baking sheets with parchment paper.

2 In a medium bowl, whisk together the flour, baking soda, baking powder, and salt.

3 In the bowl of a stand mixer fitted with the paddle attachment, beat the butter on medium speed until creamy, about 2 minutes. Add the peanut butter and mix to blend.

4 Reduce the mixer speed to low and gradually add the granulated sugar and brown sugar to the butter mixture, mixing until smooth. Add the eggs, 1 at a time, and the vanilla, beating until well blended.

5 Add the flour mixture and beat until smooth. Cover and refrigerate the dough for 20 to 30 minutes.

6 Using ¼ cup of dough for each cookie, place the cookies 3 inches apart on the prepared baking sheets. Use a spatula to lightly flatten the cookies, then use the tines of a fork to make a design on top. Bake until the cookies are golden brown, rotating the pans halfway through, about 12 minutes.

7 Let the cookies cool on the baking sheets for 3 minutes before transferring them to wire racks to cool completely.

SALLIE

SALLIE MARIE RENFROE WAS my Dad's mother. All of her grandchildren called her Nanny.

The mother of nine children, Nanny was a petite lady, about 5 feet 2 inches, with light skin, crystal-clear gray eyes, soft wavy, shoulder-length hair—and always a smile.

Although Nanny only had an eighth grade education and worked for many years cleaning homes (she later enrolled in the Arm Chair Education program through which she became a nurse's assistant), I never would have known it from how much she read; every time we went for a visit, she was invariably at her kitchen table reading, most often her Bible.

Nanny and my dad helped me understand the value of "real" food. There was this natural spring in Delaware County, and whenever I was up for it they would let me tag along with them on the hour-long drive out there; I sat in the back of the car, which was filled with plastic bottles. Once we got there, we'd get in line with all the other cars to fill our jugs with water from the spring and then haul them back to Philadelphia. And every Thanksgiving and Easter, we'd make a run to the 9th Street Italian market to pick a fresh turkey or chicken and get vegetables, or we'd go to the Reading Terminal to purchase other meats from the Amish vendors. Nanny didn't believe in grocery stores or care for their processed meats or frozen or canned foods. She and her three brothers had been raised on a farm in South

Carolina, so she liked to go to the source.

Nanny grew as much as she could in a small patch of garden behind her house where there were vegetables such as string beans, tomatoes, and peas. Even though the winters could be harsh in Philadelphia, it seemed as if Nanny's vegetables grew all year round. That was her special place. I'd often see her out there in her hat digging in the soil—"a farmer in Philadelphia," as my dad likes to say—humming a religious hymn.

Nanny just loved to sing, particularly gospel music. She was on three choirs over at Wayland Temple Baptist Church. One of her favorite songs was "Jesus Loves Me." She even taught herself how to play piano.

Nanny also loved to cook. Holiday meals were a special time for her, when all of her children and grandchildren would come to sample her chicken dumplings and her wide assortment of desserts—coconut cake, sweet potato pie, jelly cake, and lemon meringue pie. Nanny even made her own bread and pie crust. All from scratch. And never with a recipe. My dad always wondered where Nanny learned to cook so well, since her own mother left the family when she was at a very young age. But being the only girl, Nanny used to cook for her brothers and her father every day. It was Nanny, of course, who taught my dad how to cook. He especially remembers, as a child, helping her make biscuits at Easter time, so that when she came home from church on Easter morning, all she had to do was put them in the oven.

That's how we remember Nanny most: reading her Bible, singing, and smiling. And even though our sour cream pound cake, flavored with a touch of rum, may not be made with farmer's market spices, like Nanny's cakes used to be, it features only the finest, freshest ingredients, baked every day, so I know she would approve.

DOUBLE-CHOCOLATE COOKIES WITH PEANUT BUTTER CHIPS

If there ever were a perfect cookie, this would be it. Although all of our cookies are soft, the amount of chocolate we add to this one gives it a little more body, but not too much crunch. One of our neighbors at the PYT Burger Shop in Northern Liberties uses these cookies to make ice cream sandwiches. Brilliant. We suggest you try that at home.

Makes: 18 cookies

---

1   Arrange the oven racks in the upper and lower thirds of the oven. Preheat the oven to 350°F. Line 3 baking sheets with parchment paper.

2   In a medium bowl, whisk together the flour, cocoa powder, baking soda, and salt.

3   In the bowl of a stand mixer fitted with the paddle attachment, beat the butter on medium speed until smooth, about 2 minutes. Add the brown sugar and granulated sugar and beat until blended. Add the eggs, 1 at a time, and the vanilla, beating until incorporated.

Active time:
30 minutes

Total time:
50 minutes

- 2½ cups all-purpose flour
- ¾ cup unsweetened dark cocoa powder
- ½ teaspoon baking soda
- ½ teaspoon regular salt
- 2 sticks (1 cup) unsalted butter, at room temperature
- 1 cup packed light brown sugar
- ¾ cup granulated sugar
- 2 large eggs
- 2 teaspoons pure vanilla extract
- 1 tablespoon buttermilk
- ¼ cup boiling water
- ¾ cup semisweet chocolate chips
- ¾ cup peanut butter chips

4 Reduce the mixer speed to low. Add the flour mixture and buttermilk to the butter mixture and beat until blended.

5 Pour ¼ cup boiling water into the dough and beat until blended. Use a wooden spoon to mix in the chocolate chips and peanut butter chips. Cover and refrigerate the dough until it is slightly firm, about 10 minutes.

6 Using ¼ cup of the dough for each cookie, place the cookies on the prepared baking sheets, spacing them 1 inch apart. Spread the cookies to 2½ inches wide using your fingers. Bake the cookies until they are set, rotating the pans halfway through, about 10 minutes.

7 Let the cookies cool on the baking sheets for 10 minutes before transferring them to a wire rack to cool completely

SOFT SUGAR COOKIES

These cookies were only available in unlimited supply around our house during the holidays. I would wait for them all year and then eat them every day for weeks—savoring each buttery bite and leaving the bright red maraschino cherry in the center for last. They are super easy to make and were the first thing I learned to bake—ensuring I wouldn't have to wait all year to enjoy them.

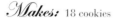

Makes: 18 cookies

1 Arrange the oven racks in the upper and lower thirds of the oven. Preheat the oven to 350°F. Line 3 baking sheets with parchment paper.

2 Sift the flour, baking powder, baking soda, and salt together into a medium bowl.

3 In the bowl of a stand mixer fitted with the paddle attachment, beat the butter and shortening on medium speed until fluffy and creamy. Slowly add the sugar, beating until light. Add the egg yolks and beat until fluffy.

4 Reduce the mixer speed to low and alternately add the flour mixture and the buttermilk, beating after each addition. Stir in the vanilla and almond extracts. Fold in the stiffly beaten egg whites.

Active time:
30 minutes

Total time:
40 minutes

7 tablespoons vegetable shortening

3 cups all-purpose flour

¾ teaspoon baking powder

½ teaspoon baking soda

½ teaspoon regular salt

4½ tablespoons unsalted butter, at room temperature

1½ cups granulated sugar

2 large egg yolks

½ cup buttermilk

1½ teaspoons pure vanilla extract

¼ teaspoon pure almond extract

2 large egg whites, stiffly beaten

10 maraschino cherries, stemmed, halved

5 Using a little less than ¼ cup of dough for each cookie, drop the dough about 3 inches apart onto the prepared baking sheets. Flatten the cookies a little with a spatula. Bake for about 7 minutes, then place half of a cherry in the center of each cookie. Return the cookies to the oven and continue to bake about 5 minutes longer.

6 Let the cookies cool on the baking sheets for a couple of minutes before transferring them to wire racks to cool completely.

WHITE CHOCOLATE MACADAMIA COOKIES

Warning: This cookie is addictive. And I'm not sure why. Is it the crunch? The salt of the macadamia nuts? The sweet of the white chocolate chunks? All of the above? Who knows. Simply put—you should plan on having more than one.

Makes: 18 cookies

1 In a medium bowl, whisk together the flour, baking soda, and salt.

2 In the bowl of a stand mixer fitted with the paddle attachment, beat the butter on medium speed until creamy, about 2 minutes.

3 Add the granulated sugar and brown sugar to the butter and beat until well blended, about 2 minutes. Add the eggs and vanilla and beat until fluffy, about 2 minutes.

4 Reduce the mixer speed to low, add the flour mixture and sour cream, and beat until blended. Use a wooden spoon to stir in the white chocolate and nuts.

5 Using ¼ cup of the dough for each cookie, roll the dough into balls, slightly flatten them and spread

Active time:
45 minutes

Total time:
1 hour and 25 minutes

3 cups all-purpose flour

1 teaspoon baking soda

1 teaspoon regular salt

7 tablespoons unsalted butter, at room temperature

¾ cup granulated sugar

¾ cup packed light brown sugar

2 large eggs

1½ teaspoons pure vanilla extract

1 tablespoon sour cream

9 ounces white chocolate, chopped

½ cup chopped macadamia nuts, toasted (see page 84)

the cookies to 2½ inches wide using your fingers, and place them on 3 parchment-lined baking sheets. Cover and refrigerate the cookies until firm, about 30 minutes.

6 Meanwhile, arrange the oven racks in the upper and lower thirds of the oven. Preheat the oven to 350°F.

7 Bake until the cookies are golden brown, rotating the pans halfway through, about 10 minutes.

8 Let the cookies cool on the baking sheets for 3 minutes before transferring them to wire racks to cool completely.

SPICE COOKIES

We entered this cookie into a local Christmas cookie competition in December 2010 to gauge response and were surprised by the number of other spice cookies in the running. Apparently, spice cookies for the holidays are more popular than we realized, so we decided to add a bit of orange to ours for a little extra zing and to make it stand out from all the rest. It has been a welcome addition to our menu ever since.

Makes: 20 cookies

Active time:
35 minutes

Total time:
1 hour and 17 minutes

2 cups all-purpose flour

1 teaspoon baking soda

1½ teaspoons ground cinnamon

1½ teaspoons ground ginger

¼ teaspoon ground allspice

¼ teaspoon ground cloves

¼ teaspoon ground black pepper

¼ teaspoon regular salt

1 stick (8 tablespoons) unsalted butter, at room temperature

¼ cup vegetable shortening

½ cup superfine sugar

⅔ cup packed light brown sugar

1 large egg

¼ cup dark molasses

1½ teaspoons pure vanilla extract

½ teaspoon pure orange extract

⅓ cup ground ginger

1 In a medium bowl, whisk together the flour, baking soda, cinnamon, ginger, allspice, cloves, pepper, and salt.

2 In the bowl of a stand mixer fitted with the paddle attachment, beat the butter and shortening on medium-high speed until blended, about 1 minute. Add the superfine sugar and brown sugar and beat until fluffy, scraping the bowl as necessary, about 3 minutes. Add the egg, molasses, vanilla, and orange extract and beat until smooth.

3 Gradually add the flour mixture, 1 cup at a time, and beat until blended. Cover and refrigerate the cookie dough until firm, about 45 minutes.

4 Meanwhile, arrange the oven racks in the upper and lower thirds of the oven. Preheat the oven to 350°F. Line two baking sheets with parchment paper.

5 Using ¼ cup of dough for each cookie, roll the dough into balls. Space the cookies 2 inches apart on the prepared baking sheets. Use your fingers to slightly flatten the cookies and sprinkle them with ginger. Bake the cookies until they are golden brown, rotating the pans halfway through, about 10 minutes.

6 Let the cookies cool on the baking sheets for 3 minutes before transferring them to wire racks to cool completely.

GERMAN CHOCOLATE CREAM CHEESE BROWNIES

My mom used to include these in her annual Christmas cookie packages. Or at least she tried to—my dad and I used to pilfer a few here and there when she wasn't looking. Although, as you know, I'm not a chocolate fan, I could not resist these—especially not the cheesecake topping or all of the tasty, crunchy walnuts inside the brownie bottom.

Makes: 14 brownies

1 Preheat the oven to 350°F. Coat a 9x13x2-inch baking pan with 1 tablespoon of butter.

2 In the bowl of a stand mixer fitted with the paddle attachment, beat the cream cheese on medium speed until light and fluffy, scraping the bowl as necessary, about 3 minutes. Gradually add ½ cup of the sugar and 2 tablespoons of the flour, beating until blended. Add 2 eggs and 1 teaspoon of the vanilla and beat until smooth. Set the cream cheese batter aside.

3 In a medium bowl, whisk together the remaining 1½ cups of flour, baking powder, and salt. Set the flour mixture aside.

Active time:
40 minutes

Total time:
1 hour and 5 minutes

- 1 tablespoon plus 2½ sticks (1¼ cups) unsalted butter, at room temperature
- 11 ounces Philadelphia® cream cheese, at room temperature
- 2¼ cups granulated sugar
- 2 tablespoons plus 1½ cups all-purpose flour
- 6 large eggs
- 3 teaspoons pure vanilla extract
- ½ teaspoon baking powder
- ¼ teaspoon regular salt
- 8 ounces German chocolate, melted
- ½ cup chopped pecans, toasted (see page 84)

4 In another bowl of a stand mixer fitted with the paddle attachment, beat the 2½ sticks of butter on medium speed until smooth, about 2 minutes. Gradually add the remaining 1¾ cups of sugar, scraping the bowl as necessary and beating until light and fluffy, about 2 minutes.

5 Add the remaining 4 eggs, 2 at a time, beating until blended. Add the remaining 2 teaspoons of vanilla and the melted chocolate and beat until smooth.

6 Reduce the mixer speed to low. Add the flour mixture, ½ cup at a time, to the chocolate batter, beating until blended. Stir in the pecans.

7 Pour the chocolate batter into the prepared pan. Use an offset spatula to spread the cream cheese batter over the chocolate batter. Cut through the mixture with a fork several times to create a marbled design.

8 Bake until a wooden pick inserted into the center comes out with a few moist crumbs attached, 30 to 35 minutes.

9 Transfer the pan of brownies to a wire rack to cool completely. Cut into squares.

TRIPLE-CHOCOLATE NUT BROWNIES

This is our take on a classic brownie. It is simple, but delicious. Just add a cold glass of milk and you are set.

Makes: 14 brownies

1 Preheat the oven to 350°F. Coat a 9x13x2-inch baking pan with 1 tablespoon of butter.

2 In a large microwave-safe glass bowl, microwave the 2½ sticks of butter and chocolate together for 15 to 20 seconds, then stir and repeat until melted.

3 Gradually stir the granulated sugar and brown sugar into the butter mixture until blended. Add the eggs and vanilla and mix until smooth, about 1 minute.

4 In a medium bowl, whisk together the flour, cocoa powder, and salt. Add the flour mixture, ½ cup at a time, to the chocolate batter and mix until smooth.

5 By hand, stir in ½ cup each of the nuts and chocolate chips. Pour the batter into the prepared pan. Sprinkle the remaining nuts and chocolate chips on top.

6 Bake until a wooden pick inserted into the center comes out with a few moist crumbs attached, 20 to 25 minutes. Transfer the pan of brownies to a wire rack to cool completely. Cut into squares.

Active time:
25 minutes

Total time:
50 minutes

- 1 tablespoon plus 2½ sticks (1¼ cups) unsalted butter
- 4 ounces unsweetened chocolate, chopped
- 1¼ cups granulated sugar
- 1 cup packed light brown sugar
- 4 large eggs
- 2 teaspoons pure vanilla extract
- 1¼ cups all-purpose flour
- 4 tablespoons unsweetened dark cocoa powder
- ½ teaspoon regular salt
- 1 cup chopped walnuts or pecans, toasted (see page 84)
- 1 cup semisweet chocolate chips

THELMA

THELMA BOLTEN WAS ONE of my dad's older sisters, but she was more than a sister-in-law to my mom—she became one of her very best friends. Mom and Aunt Thelma met back in the early 1970s when my mom and dad were just kids in high school. Aunt Thelma, already married, was the cool big sister and the life of the party, while my mom was quite the opposite at the time—quiet and introverted. But somehow the two hit it off—likely because Aunt Thelma had a way of clicking with everyone.

Aunt Thelma, at a tiny 4 feet 11 inches, was fair skinned with a short pixie cut that she kept colored golden blonde. With a beaming smile and an infectious, friendly laugh, she was always hosting a party or a barbecue. Every New Year's Eve, she would have a big open house where people filled up every inch of the two-bedroom, second-floor apartment that she shared with Uncle Sonny on the corner of Divinity Street and Chester Avenue in Southwest Philadelphia. Upwards of forty or fifty people at a time would be there—in the kitchen, in the living room, in the bedrooms—but it never felt crowded or uncomfortable. That's because Aunt Thelma made everyone feel at home.

Aunt Thelma made real soul food too, the kind people don't cook anymore, like chitterlings, pig's feet, black-eyed peas, fried chicken, potato salad, ham, and greens. Her chitterlings were so popular that she would put out little storage containers so guests could take some home with them. For New Year's Eve, she would start preparing as early as Christmas, because cooking chitterlings—and especially cleaning them—is a skill that requires meticulous attention and a lot of time. And she did it all by herself. Happily.

In the summertime, Aunt Thelma would host a huge cookout in West Fairmount Park, the same spot every year, across from the Shofuso Japanese House. Often she would pick a big holiday like Memorial Day, Independence Day, or Labor Day, but some years it would end up on a regular weekend, and family and friends came in droves. We'd be out there for hours—playing games, riding bikes, dancing, and laughing. And there was always more food than you could eat. Aunt Thelma was so concerned about having enough food that she would often overbuy. Cousin Karen, Thelma's daughter, jokes that eventually she had to start doing the grocery shopping to keep Aunt Thelma "from spending too much money."

But Aunt Thelma's generosity went far beyond holidays and special occasions. For thirty years, every Friday, she left her job at the 30th Street post office and spent the night with her mother, my Nanny, to help her clean her house and take care of her business. And one of my last memories of Aunt Thelma, who died at a young age of fifty-eight, after battling breast cancer for two decades, was the day I went to see her before starting my summer clerkship at one of the law firms downtown. By then, she was so weak that she was getting nurse care and sleeping in a hospital bed, but she told Cousin Karen to grab her purse and give me carfare so that I could get to work the next day. That was just her way.

All through my childhood, I remember jumping out of my dad's 1978 white Volvo as one of my parents yelled up to that second-floor apartment, "Hey, Thelma, come on down" or "throw down the key." Down the key would fall, and up the flight of stairs we would go. We've dedicated our chocolate cake with caramel coconut filling (page 82) to a woman who not only was my mom's best friend, but, in essence, was a kindred spirit to all.

LEMON BARS

When I think of lemon bars, I think of spring breezes and Easter gatherings. These bars are the perfect way to top off an Easter brunch table—they are fruity and light, and you can cut them into small, bite-size pieces just in case your guests have already overindulged on brunch.

Makes: 21 bars

1   Preheat the oven to 350°F. Lightly coat a 9x13x2-inch baking pan with 1 tablespoon of butter.

2   For the crust, in a medium bowl, whisk together the flour, granulated sugar, and brown sugar. Add the 2 sticks of butter and mix until a dough forms.

3   Pat the dough into the prepared pan and bake until golden brown, about 25 minutes. Set aside.

4   For the filling, in the bowl of a stand mixer fitted with the paddle attachment, beat the cream cheese and salt on medium speed until smooth, about 3 minutes. Gradually add the granulated sugar, flour, and baking powder and beat until blended.

5   Add the eggs, lemon juice, and lemon zest and beat until well blended, scraping the bowl as necessary. Do not overmix.

Active time:
35 minutes

Total time:
1 hour and 30 minutes

CRUST

1 tablespoon plus 2 sticks (1 cup) unsalted butter, at room temperature

1½ cups all-purpose flour

½ cup granulated sugar

½ cup packed light brown sugar

FILLING

One 8-ounce package Philadelphia® cream cheese, at room temperature

¼ teaspoon regular salt

½ cup granulated sugar

2 tablespoons all-purpose flour

½ teaspoon baking powder

2 large eggs, lighly beaten

3 tablespoons fresh lemon juice

2 teaspoons freshly grated lemon zest

6 Pour the filling over the crust and bake until a wooden pick inserted into the center comes out clean, 30 to 35 minutes.

7 Transfer the pan to a wire rack to cool completely. When cool, cut into bars.

INDEX

Page numbers in *italics* indicate photos